Chinese Philosophy

In this illustrated introduction Wen Haiming explores the characteristics of different philosophers in Chinese history and distinguishes the "Chinese philosophical sensibility" motivating their thoughts. Employing Western philosophical categories to describe significant issues in the history of philosophy, Wen Haiming considers Chinese political philosophy in the pre-Qin era, Chinese metaphysics from Han to Tang dynasties, Chinese epistemology from Song to Ming dynasties and modern Chinese-Western comparative philosophy. *Chinese Philosophy* provides a clear, accessible conception of the Chinese philosophical sensibility and its evolution throughout history.

Introductions to Chinese Culture

The thirty volumes in the Introductions to Chinese Culture series provide accessible overviews of particular aspects of Chinese culture written by a noted expert in the field concerned. The topics covered range from architecture to archaeology, from mythology and music to martial arts. Each volume is lavishly illustrated in full color and will appeal to students requiring an introductory survey of the subject, as well as to more general readers.

Wen Haiming

CHINESE
PHILOSOPHY

CAMBRIDGE
UNIVERSITY PRESS

CAMBRIDGE UNIVERSITY PRESS
Cambridge, New York, Melbourne, Madrid, Cape Town,
Singapore, São Paulo, Delhi, Tokyo, Mexico City

Cambridge University Press
The Edinburgh Building, Cambridge CB2 8RU, UK

Published in the United States of America by Cambridge University Press,
New York

www.cambridge.org
Information on this title: www.cambridge.org/9780521186766

Originally published by China Intercontinental Press as
Chinese Philosophy (9787508513195) in 2010

© China Intercontinental Press 2010

This updated edition is published by Cambridge University Press
with the permission of China Intercontinental Press under
the China Book International programme 　.

For more information on the China Book International programme, please visit
http://www.cbi.gov.cn/wisework/content/10005.html

Cambridge University Press retains copyright in its own contributions
to this updated edition

© Cambridge University Press 2012

First published 2012

Printed and bound in China by C&C Offset Printing Co., Ltd

A catalogue record for this publication is available from the British Library

ISBN   978-0-521-18676-6 Paperback

Contents

Introduction: What is Chinese Philosophy? 1

***Zhouyi*: The Starting Point of Chinese Philosophy** 7
A Mystical and Profound Classic 8
From *Taiji* to Eight Trigrams 11
The Philosophy of *Zhouyi* 14

Chinese Political Philosophy: Pre-Qin Philosophers 21
Confucius (Kongzi): Family Reverence as the Root of Humanity 22
Mencius (Mengzi): Governing the State with Humane Love 31
Laozi: The Great *Dao* is like Water 38
Zhuangzi: Wandering at ease without Self 48
Mozi and other Pre-Qin Thinkers 55
Xunzi's Political Theory 58
Han Fei's Art of Rulership 60
Sunzi's *Art of War* 62

Chinese Metaphysics: Interpretations of the World from Han to Tang Dynasties 67
Chinese Cosmology in the Han Dynasty 68
The Ontology of Being and Nothingness in the Wei-Jin Dynasties 74
Chinese Metaphysics of Emptiness (*Sunyata*): Buddhism in the Sui and Tang Dynasties 84
Chan Buddhism: Enlightening Buddhist Wisdom 97

Chinese Epistemology: Song-Ming Philosophers on the Relationship between Mind-Heart and Things/Events 105

From Han Yu to Zhang Zai 106

The Cheng Brothers and the "Luo School" 114

Zhu Xi: Extinguishing Human Desires in order to keep Heavenly Li 117

Lu Jiuyuan: The Cosmos does not exist without Mind 122

Wang Yangming: Nothing is outside one's Mind 124

The *Dao* of Chinese Philosophy: Its Sustainment and Creativity 131

Three Philosophers between the Ming and Qing Dynasties 132

Modern Chinese Philosophy as responses to Western Philosophies 138

Modern Chinese Philosophy: New Confucianism and East-West Comparative Philosophy 145

Hu Shi, Fung Yu-lan, and the discipline of Modern Chinese Philosophy 146

Xiong Shili and New Confucianism 148

Contemporary East-West Comparative Philosophy 152

Appendix I: Table of Key Philosophical Terms 157

Appendix II: Timeline of Chinese and Western Philosophies 160

Appendix III: Chronological Table of the Chinese Dynasties 165

Introduction
What is Chinese Philosophy?

The relationship between human beings and the world is the central concern for Chinese philosophers. Chinese philosophy includes the use of wisdom in regard to human life, and various arguments regarding the perception of the world. Many Chinese philosophical texts, such as *The Book of Changes* (*Zhouyi* 周易), discuss the relationship between *tian* (*tian* 天/heavens) and human beings. We might say that traditional Chinese thinkers tried to help people live good lives so they could enjoy their single journey of living existence.

In the eyes of traditional Chinese philosophers, people naturally puzzle about life and the world, but this is all derived from their misunderstanding of *dao* (*dao* 道/way-making). *Dao* is the road we walk in life, which stands analogously to a person's behavior and development. Throughout this journey, we remain unclear of its direction because we lack understanding of our own nature, or *xing* (*xing* 性/nature). Thus, the basic philosophical inquiries of Western philosophers, such as social, political and cosmic problems concerning life and knowledge, are also those of Chinese philosophers. It is in the process of answering these fundamental philosophical problems that Chinese philosophers developed a unique "Chinese philosophical sensibility."

Generally speaking, the Chinese philosophical tradition can be divided according to its different periods: pre-Qin philosophy, studies of Classics in the Han Dynasty, Neo-Daoism in the

Wei-Jin dynasties, Buddhism in the Sui-Tang dynasties, Song-Ming Neo-Confucianism, and modern philosophy. Accordingly, there are different methods of philosophical narrative and hermeneutical methodologies based on the unfolding process of questions, categories, and philosophical concepts. It is necessary to incorporate methods of analysis, critical thinking and abstract philosophical narrative into historical narrative, and to employ a

Dao – an important concept in Chinese philosophy.

systematic "philosophical" analysis of Chinese philosophical thinking and the scope of its concerns. The general characteristics of ancient Chinese theories can be difficult to grasp, making it very difficult for readers to understand the reason why these theories are deemed "philosophy." In fact, ancient Chinese thinkers display a variety of philosophical perspectives.

In light of this, this book aims to explore the philosophical characteristics of different philosophers in various periods, and to distinguish the philosophical sensibility motivating their thought. In doing so, I employ Western philosophical categories to describe different issues in Chinese philosophy, so as to provide readers with a clear conception of Chinese philosophical sensibility and the evolution of various schools.

The philosophy of *The Book of Changes* (*Zhouyi*) is the source of Chinese philosophical thought. *Zhouyi* philosophy not only serves as the basis for different philosophical schools throughout history, but also as the ultimate origin of Chinese philosophical sensibility. *Zhouyi* philosophy provides us with a systematic understanding of political philosophy, metaphysics and epistemology, as well as the ethics and aesthetics of Chinese philosophy. This book aims to discuss how the political philosophy, metaphysics, and epistemology of *Zhouyi* evolved throughout the history of Chinese philosophy.

The central debate of pre-Qin philosophers was the discussion of social order, though pre-Qin philosophers also covered most aspects of the Chinese philosophical realm and set up the basic paradigm of philosophical discourse. Chinese philosophy began with Confucianism. Confucius' idea that "family reverence (*xiao* 孝) is the root of human beings" provided the origin and focus of Confucian political philosophy, and sparked most philosophical debates in pre-Qin politics. Mencius advocates "ruling states by humanity and love" and launches the practical dimension of Confucian political philosophy based on "humanity" (*ren*仁), which provides a theoretical premise for the epistemology of the Song-Ming dynasties.

Confucius raises the basic questions of political philosophy, and other philosophers answer his questions from diverse angles. Laozi holds that leadership should remain fluid in character, maintaining "*dao* is like water" as his central theme. He discusses the philosophical meaning of *dao* and the possibility of turning it into a reality. Zhuangzi endorses "wandering at ease without oneself" as the ultimate ideal of a politician. Daoism covers the theoretical levels of political philosophy, and serves as a reference for cultivating oneself and going forth with one's life-long pursuit. The *Great Learning* (*Daxue*), *Focusing the Familiar* (*Zhongyong*) and the four chapters of *Guanzi* explicitly discuss methods of cultivating oneself, and mention how doing so might influence others in society.

However, the greatest impact on traditional Chinese society comes from in-depth debates on political philosophy, which covers nearly everything from pacifism to military strategy. Mozi's political philosophy, for example, promotes anti-war sentiments and universal love. Xunzi's political theory takes human nature to be evil, directly opposing Mencius' doctrine describing human nature as good. Xunzi argues that the teaching of ritual and music may help to transform the evil nature of human beings, and that a ruler should legally control his nation from the inside while maintaining proper ritual from the outside. Han Fei, the synthesizer of legalist schools, holds that only with the combination of powerful propensity (*shi* 势), legal regulation (*fa* 法) and the art of rulership (*shu* 术) can a ruler control a state. These dialectical political arguments are also prevalent in military strategy and thought.

The Chinese worldview is exemplified in the cosmology of the Han Dynasty, the ontology of the Wei-Jin dynasties, and Buddhism in the Sui-Tang dynasties. There are five dimensions in Han Dynasty cosmology. Originally, Confucian scholars and fortune-tellers combined the theories of *yin-yang* (*yinyang* 阴阳) and *wuxing* (*wuxing* 五行/five processes) to form a shared diagram of the cosmos. Numbers and images are used to create cosmological diagrams, and the peak of this practice is found in the supplement of *Zhouyi* (*Yiwei*). Dong Zhongshu gives the cosmos a human identity and creates the theory that human beings are the replica of *tian*, and thus can mutually resonate from one another. The Daoist tradition regards the cosmos as a tool for self-cultivation, and a symbol of immortality. This later becomes typical of Chinese religious systems. Baihutong interprets the cosmos from a moral perspective, and defines three guiding codes (*gang*) and five constant virtues (*chang*), which has a strong influence on traditional Confucian society. Huan Tang and Wang Chong interpret the cosmos from the perspectives of nature (*xing*) and *qi* (*qi* 气/psycho-material force), and point out the relationship between the original cosmological *qi* and human nature.

The main topics of Wei-Jin metaphysics are "being" and "non-being." Wang Bi holds that "non-being" is the source of "being," and Pei Wei brought forth a treatise on "being." Guo Xiang deems things to be "lone-transforming" in a remote "dark-joining" context, and thus things can be said to arise as they obliterate.

In the Sui and Tang dynasties, the central topic of Chinese Buddhism is "emptiness" (*kong* 空/sunyata) which is laid out in the Mah,y,na ("Great Vehicle") School. For example, the Hua-yan School maintains that ontological existence and phenomena are continuous, an idea indicative of the Chinese understanding of the world.

The Song Dynasty philosophers change their focus to epistemology during the peak of metaphysical study. They discuss much on the relationship between mind and things, and develop a typical system of epistemology with Chinese characteristics. The foundation of Song-Ming epistemology comes from the epistemology of Chan Buddhism, as well as Li Ao's theory of recovering human nature, which traces back to the Mencius doctrine expounding the goodness of human nature. Zhou Dunyi presents an epistemology based on *cheng* (creativity); Shao Yong states a theory of "viewing things from things themselves;" Zhang Zai declares that extending one's mind allows one to embrace all things under heaven; Cheng Hao avers that a human being can live a natural life by thoroughly fulfilling his or her natural tendency. Cheng Yi contends that the heavenly patterns (*tianli* 天理) are outside our minds, providing a theoretical foundation for Zhu Xi's investigation of things. Lu Jiuyuan takes mind and the cosmos to be continuous, which was succeeded by Wang Yangming's view that nothing is outside one's mind. Thus, Song-Ming epistemology reaches further in depth than any previous philosophical study.

Huang Zongxi, Fang Yizhi and Wang Fuzhi are three major thinkers between the Ming and Qing dynasties. Their guardianship of the transiting *dao* of Chinese philosophy set a theoretical foundation for the dialogue between Chinese and Western philosophies. They succeeded and developed the epistemological achievement of the Song-Ming period. Huang Zongxi, for example, realizes that "it is mind that covers all between heaven and earth." Fang Yizhi contends that "there is no mind if things are left out, and there is nothing if mind is left out." Wang Fuzhi maintains that the ability of realization needs to be consistent with the object of realization. All in all, these two developed Chinese philosophical sensibility to its thorough logical analysis.

Modern Chinese philosophy evolves through communication between Chinese and Western cultures. Chinese philosophical sensibility continues in Sino-Western comparative studies. Hu Shi and Fung Yu-lan apply the methodology of Western philosophy to rearrange Chinese philosophical materials. Xiong Shili establishes an original philosophical system by synthesizing Western traditions, and his philosophy has had a strong impact on the growing relationship between Chinese and Western philosophies.

Zhouyi:

The Starting Point of Chinese Philosophy

*T*he *Book of Changes* (*Zhouyi* 周易) is the fundamental resource of Chinese philosophy. All sub-divisions of Chinese philosophy, such as political philosophy, metaphysics, epistemology, even ethics and aesthetics are rooted in the philosophy of *The Book of Changes*. It is *Zhouyi* that shapes the unique Chinese philosophical awareness. In other words, the ultimate origin of Chinese philosophical awareness is rooted in the exclusive thinking paradigm involved in the *Zhouyi* philosophical system.

A Mystical and Profound Classic

Zhouyi is a book written to reveal the *dao* of things changing between heavens and earth, which in ancient Chinese refers to the world as a whole. It aims to help things flourish and facilitate human affairs. The authors of the *Zhouyi* imitate the changing myriad things in the cosmos by applying a structure of hexagrams and images based on their observation of natural changes over a period of 1,500 years, from 2000 BC to 500 BC.

Yi in the *Zhouyi* has three meanings: (1) mutability; (2) immutability; (3) ease and simplicity. Mutability or transforming indicates that everything is forever changing and the *Zhouyi* is a book about the philosophy of change. Immutability accounts for the relatively unchanged *dao* that exists though things are always flowing. Both the *dao* of nature and human affairs might have a character of immutability, just like the patterns in handling things and the principle of moving things. The third connotation of *yi* is ease and simplicity because the *dao* of *yi* is easy to understand, and simple to be put into practice even if things constantly change, making the *Zhouyi* complicated in nature.

The *Zhouyi* is composed of the following elements: numbers, images, trigrams, hexagrams and words.

The basis of the *Zhouyi* is its unique philosophy of numbers. It is said in the *Great Appendix* (*dazhuan* 大传): "The Yellow River brought forth the *He-tu*, and Luo River brought forth the *Luo-shu*, and sages imitated them to create *The Book of Changes*." In the ancient legend, the dragon-horse jumped out of Yellow River with He-tu on its back, and the divine tortoise floated on the Luo River with *Luo-shu* on its back. When Fu Xi saw them, he created the eight trigrams according to its philosophy of numbers. The *He-tu* and *Luo-shu* were formed through the inter-changing of the natural numbers of heaven and earth. Odd (*yang*) numbers move and even (*yin*) numbers remain stable. *He-tu* is formed by

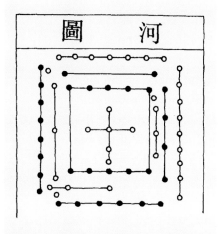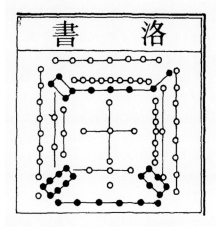

He-tu and *Luo-shu*

numbers one to ten, and *Luo-shu* is formed by numbers one to nine.

He-tu and *Luo-shu* inform people to separate *yin* from *yang* based on the odd and even nature of numbers. The system of numbers and tri/hexagrams is balanced in the *Zhouyi* and its philosophy of numbering can be explained through *Luo-shu*, which discloses the relationship between numbers and tri/hexagrams. This philosophy of numbering displays the rigor and efficiency of the philosophical reasoning of ancient Chinese people, though it lacks the structure of Western analytical philosophizing.

The appliance of numbers in the *Zhouyi* system is involved in its method of divination, calculating a tri/hexagram over intricate steps.

This image is the basis for constructing the *Zhouyi* into a book. *Xiang* 象 (image) means to imitate and represent. Each trigram represents a kind of thing or event in the heavens-and-earth. The ancient people considered there to be eight kinds of basic things in the world, and characterized them to be heavens, earth, thunder, wind, water, fire, mountains and lakes. Each is symbolized by a trigram: Qian 乾, Kun 坤, Zhen 震, Xun 巽, Kan 坎, Li 离, Gen 艮, Dui 兑.

If one wants to comprehend the tangible image of the eight trigrams, one needs to clarify the image indications via *Explaining Trigrams* (*shuogua* 说卦) of the *Great Appendix*, an article that explicates images. It discusses images and directions of the pre-heavens and post-heavens trigrams, and explains how each symbolizes a series of objects or events.

Zhouyi was created by people who lived in the central area around the Yellow River for many generations. The basic component of the trigrams is the undivided line "-," i.e., *yang/strong* line, or broken line "- -," i.e., *yin/soft* line. The *yang* line represents *yangqi*, and the *yin* line represents *yinqi*. The communication of *yinqi* and *yangqi* produce myriad things. The crossing of three lines constitutes one of eight trigrams, and the duplication of one trigram with another forms one of the sixty-four hexagrams. The first of the sixty-four hexagrams is Hexagram Qian, which is composed of six yang lines; and the second hexagram is Hexagram Kun, which is made up of six yin lines.

The words of the *Zhouyi* have two sections: one is the *Classic* (*jing* 经) and the other is the *Commentaries* (*zhuan* 传). It is said that the *Classic* was created by both Fu Xi and King Wen of Zhou. The *Classic* is less than 5,000 words, and it is ancient, obscure, succinct and profound. It explains each line in each hexagram. Over time, numerous commentaries have been developed for the *Classic* alone. *Zhouyi* is a book made through the process of observing images and attaching words. In ancient times, philosophers hung woodcuts representing hexagrams, and read images through the trigrams and changing lines. The trigram *Qian*, for example, symbolizes *tian*, ruler and father, and its crossing line movements intrigue more moving images. Hexagrams and lines are thus produced via the transcription of these ancient observations.

The *Great Appendix* elucidates the *Classic*, so it is alleged to be its supplement. To understand the *Zhouyi* today, we must rely on the *Great Appendix*. According to the traditional view, the author of the *Great Appendix* was Confucius, who read *Zhouyi* so diligently in his later years that the leather bond of his bamboo slips broke several times. Confucius was afraid that people after him might not be able to understand the meaning of the *Zhouyi*, so he compiled the ten articles of the *Great Appendix*, which is called "Ten Wings," in the light of their accompaniment to the *Classic*. The *Attaching Statements* are a philosophical elucidation of the *Classic* with profound philosophical meanings. *Explaining Trigrams* (*Shuogua* 说卦) explains the symbolism of the eight trigrams and their characteristics.

From *Taiji* to Eight Trigrams

From the perspective of existence, *Zhouyi* considers everything in the world as having a *taiji*, and purports the universe as a whole to be a *taiji* also. From the perspective of evolution, the *taiji* is the starting point of the universe. It is said in the *Attaching Statements*: "In the Yi there is the Great Ultimate (*taiji*) which produces the Two Forms. The Two Forms generate the Four Images, and these Four Images give birth to the eight trigrams." This alludes to the evolution of cosmological process, and it also suggests that things or events can be divided into different parts, but are continuous through parts and a whole.

The diagram to represent the Great Ultimate is the *Taiji* Diagram, which is composed of a white half circle and black half circle, with a moving line splitting them apart in between. Both half circles look like fishes, so the *Taiji* Diagram is also called *"yin-yang* fishes." It assumes the universe starts with an original *qi*, which is malleable to transform into *yinqi* and *yangqi. Yangqi* is light and clear, so it rises to be *tian* (heavens), while *yinqi* is heavy and dirty, falling down to be earth. This is the cosmological starting process of the heavens and earth. In other words, everything is a *taiji* (great ultimate) when whole, and can be divided into *yin* and *yang.*

Taiji Diagram

"The Two Forms generate the Four Images" means that both *yin* and the *yang* forms generate one *yin* and one *yang* independently, and the Four Images come into being: *taiyang, shaoyin, shaoyang, taiyin.* Each of these Four Images gives birth to one *yin* and one *yang*, thus shaping the eight trigrams.

There are two groups of the Eight Trigrams: the Pre-Heavens Eight Trigrams and the Post-Heavens Eight Trigrams. The sequence of the Pre-Heavens Eight Trigrams is: *Qian* 乾, *Dui* 兑, *Li* 离, *Zhen* 震, *Xun* 巽, *Kan* 坎, *Gen* 艮, *Kun* 坤, and each of them resonates with a fundamental thing-image in the universe: *tian* (heavens), lakes, fire, thunder, wind, water, mountains and earth.

The Pre-Heavens Eight Trigrams (*xiantian bagua*).

The Pre-Heavens Eight Trigrams represent the initial circumstances of nature. It is said in *Explaining Trigrams* (*Shuogua* 说卦), "Heavens and earth determine the direction. The forces of mountains and lakes are continuous. Thunder and wind arise from one another. Water and fire do not combat each other. Thus are the eight trigrams intermingled." This represents the Pre-Heavens Eight Trigrams. For the ancients, the Pre-Heavens Eight Trigrams symbolized the original proto-types of the world. However, after the original *qi* was

The Post-Heavens Eight Trigrams (*houtian bagua*).

divided, its nature remained the same, and the Great Ultimate evolved into Two Forms, Four Images, and Eight Trigrams. It is an example of the continuity of the one and the many that nature persists through various modes.

The Post-Heavens Eight Trigrams (*houtian bagua* 后天八卦) is the rearrangement of the Pre-Heavens Eight Trigrams. Sima Qian, the Han Dynasty historian, writes that "King Wen of Zhou performed *Zhouyi* when he was in prison." Ji Chang, the King of Zhou was the leader of the Zhou State at the end of the Shang Dynasty. He was imprisoned by King Zhou of Yin in the City of Youli for seven years merely on account of his "frankness." King Zhou of Yin murdered Ji Kao, the elder son of King Wen, chopped his corpse, made bread with it and forced King Wen to eat it. The old King Wen, at the age of eighty-two, was forced to eat his son's flesh while weeping. He devoted the remainder of his life to the trigrams, and rearranged the Pre-Heavens Eight Trigrams of Fu Xi to be the Post-Heavens Eight Trigrams, later named after him.

The Post-Heavens Eight Trigrams start from the East, and are arranged clockwise. The Post-Heavens Eight Trigrams correspond with the directions and seasons, as well as the movement of the Big Dipper. Therefore, the appliance of the *Zhouyi* is based on the Post-Heavens Eight Trigrams and extends to ancient knowledge of astrology, geography, music, military strategy, mathematics, medicine, *feng shui* and even pills of immortality. The Post-Heavens Eight Trigrams created by King Wen of Zhou are said to be the theoretical foundation of the ancient Chinese pragmatic culture.

Zhouyi was created in the area of the Yellow River. Ancients observed the changing phenomena in the sky and on the earth over thousands of years, and developed a theory of Five Processes (*wuxing*)

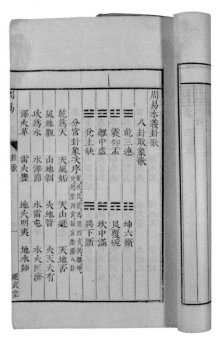

To aid memory, Zhu Xi wrote a song of corresponding images of the eight trigrams in his *Original Meaning of Zhouyi*.

in which one produces and conquers another based on living experience. Wood, Fire, Earth, Metal and Water correspond with the four directions and the center. In the sequence of wood-fire-earth-metal-water, each is the cause of its successor, and each destroys its successor's successor. In other words, the sequence of generating is wood-fire-earth-metal-water-wood; whereas the sequence of destruction is: wood-earth-water-fire-metal-wood. These patterns help to explain the Post-Heavens Eight Trigrams.

The Philosophy of *Zhouyi*

For *Zhouyi* philosophy, *dao* is moving between the heavens and the earth. *Zhouyi's dao* of *tian* is embodied in human social relationships, and penetrates to the *dao* of ordinary things that are engaged with human beings.

The *dao* of *Zhouyi* holds, "the movement of one yin and one yang is the *dao*." One starts from *dao* to fulfill one's nature and thoroughly understand one's destiny. The *Zhouyi* stresses penetration into the minute changes of things, and reveals the continuity between mind and events. The *Zhouyi* clarifies human affairs through the understanding of the *dao* of *tian*. It encourages people to illuminate the *dao* of *tian*, and thoroughly disclose the magically transforming patterns of complex human affairs. In this way, people may come to understand the time and space in which they are located, and enhance their power to manipulate the changing world.

Zhouyi philosophy maintains that everything in the world has both *yin* and *yang*. The movement of *yin* and *yang* forms the *dao*. The *yin* and *yang* are the basic symbol of the *Zhouyi*, and can be illustrated by the *yin-yang* fishes in the *Taiji* Diagram. The *yin* and *yang* mutually contain one another, and transform to be the other. The ancients tried to tell us that all things and events contain both *yin* and *yang*, which are forever transforming.

Everything is a continuity of *yin* and *yang*, which cannot be viewed as separate oppositions. *Yin* and *yang* stand relative to one another. For example, if the front is *yang*, then the back is *yin*; if the up is yang, then the down is *yin*; if the left is *yang*, then the right is *yin*. *Zhouyi* puts forth a *yin-yang* contextualizing paradigm quite different from Western models of separate opposing parts.

According to *Zhouyi*, what follows the development of a moving *dao* is the good, and what this *dao* fulfills is natural. Good is the original character of the heavenly moving *dao*, and nature is the concrete beings that *dao* has concretized to be particular individuals. Thus, nature is the root within which every being in reality exists. The *Zhouyi's* structure linking *dao* to nature to destiny provides an explanation for the concrete existence of the whole world. Its theory in itself presents a dynamic metaphysical system full of creativity.

In understanding the continuity of mind and events, most Chinese philosophers do not apply analytical methodology in solving epistemological problems like their Western counterparts. Most Chinese philosophers seem to feel that logical deduction does not help in understanding the epistemological object. Many Chinese philosophers opted to face things or events directly. They felt that the world could only be understood in totality by intuitive thought.

Generally speaking, people have difficulty fathoming their own time and existence, and can only conceive of them through philosophical speculation. *Zhouyi* is a book that assists people in realizing their own time and position. The lines in a hexagram illustrate time and space so as to aid people in understanding their own context. The time and space in which people live are changing, as are their propensities and social status. It is useful for one to understand the proper strategies with regard to these variables. People cannot transcend the time and space in which they are situated, and they need to pay attention to them when acting. In everyone's living environment, the outer conditions create an irreversible effect. A person as an acting agent should be habituated to his or her environment. *Zhouyi* informs people that one should comprehend the time and space he or she is situated in, remain aware of possible outcomes, and lead the development of habitual events. Exercising a free will, the human mind will make more appropriate choices in a situated context. In this way, the *Zhouyi* illuminates the *dao* of *tian*, and thus helps people to live a better life.

The *Zhouyi* takes human beings to be a part of natural process. Human beings have been correlative to natural changes since the dawn of time. Living in the world lets one's thinking and

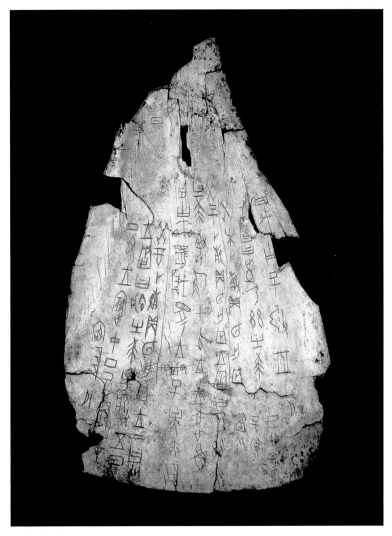

Oracle bones from the Shang Dynasty (1600-1046 BC)

behavior assume a continuous state of mind and events with self-consciousness, and the *dao* of a person's life can remain harmonious with the *dao* that nature operates.

The *Zhouyi* persuades people to assimilate themselves into the functioning state of nature. Ideally, a person's words and actions

Ancient people reading *Zhouyi*.

are harmonious with the running rhythm of the world. An agent acts according to the moving world, and should be consistent with the *dao* of heaven and earth. After a person embodies the *dao's* movement, the way he or she handles events can be harmonious with the great *dao* of heavenly movements. "Great people (*Daren*)" are those whose actions catch the rhythms of nature, those who understand the great *dao* of the cosmos, and those who enhance themselves with cosmological sensibility. If one understands the philosophical sensibility of *Zhouyi*, one's mind will improve, and one will become a "great person" with cosmological sensibility, who harmonizes with the change of the world. In doing so, a great person has the ability to manipulate the world.

The *Zhouyi* is the primary origin of yin and yang, the continuity of mind and events, as well as the continuity between heaven and human beings. The *Zhouyi* assists people in understanding a correlative relationship between human beings and the world, and pursues a harmonious relationship between the human mind and cosmological rhythms. The ancients wished to co-create along with the world they lived in. They appreciated the creativity of the myriad things, and devoted their lives to their enterprises. In short, the *Zhouyi* thinks through the *dao* of *tian* and illuminates the *dao* of human affairs as it explores the subtle and delicate continuity between heaven and human beings. It demonstrates that the *dao* of achievement flows continuous with that of *tian*.

Chinese Political Philosophy:
Pre-Qin Philosophers

In the later years of the Spring and Autumn Period (770-476 BC), the Zhou Dynasty (1046-256 BC) collapsed and only sustained itself in name. Emperors of various states fought against each other. The ritual and music of the Zhou Dynasty totally fell apart. There were no morals to regulate people's minds. The philosophers of this chaotic time naturally focused their debates on the central theme of how to recover their social system. Most philosophers were deeply concerned about people's lives, destinies and social circumstances. Philosophers cared about different aspects of the problem, as they began from various starting points, and they provided diverse or even contradictory answers. Thus, the philosophical thinking of the pre-Qin era was mainly presented in the form of political philosophy.

Confucius (Kongzi): Family Reverence as the Root of Humanity

Confucius' (Kongzi, 551-479 BC) personal name was Qiu. He was born during the Spring and Autumn Period in the state of Lu, in present Shandong Province. He was a descendent of the ducal house of the state of Song, a family once associated with the royal house of the Shang Dynasty. While his father was elderly, his mother was very young when Confucius was born. Hence, the great historian Sima Qian declared the relationship of Confucius' parents an informal one. Despite the family's nobility, Confucius and his relatives had a penurious existence. Confucius lost his father at the age of three, and his mother passed away at the age of seventeen. He had to face the world alone after his mother passed away. He studied hard while working diligently to make a living, holding jobs including storehouse clerk and shepherd. However, Confucius did not give in to the suffering of life. He set his mind on education and continued to study. At about thirty, he first began to take on disciples. After his lifetime endeavor, Confucius became the creator of the Confucian School of thought.

When Duke Ding of Lu was in power, Confucius took various government positions, such as the governor of Zhongdu City, and Minister of Public Construction. When he was

Confucius by Ma Yuan of the Southern Song Dynasty (1127-1279).

Confucius rearranging the *Book of Poems* and other works.

The Six Confucian Classics

The Six Confucian Classics are said to have been composed by Confucius (Kongzi 孔子) himself, but the main part of the corpus was written or at least compiled in the Han Dynasty, when Confucianism became the official state philosophy. The books include the *Yijing* "Book of Changes," the *Shujing* (书经, or *Shangshu* 尚书) "Book of Documents," the *Shijing* (诗经) "Book of Poetry," the *Liji* (礼记) "Records of Rites" and the *Chunqiu* (春秋) "Spring and Autumn Annals," and the lost *Yuejing* (乐经) "Book of Music," which might now be part of the *Liji Classic as Yueji* (乐记)"Record of Music." In the Han Dynasty, the "Book of Rites" was referred to the *Yili* (仪礼) "Etiquette and Rites," and in the Song Dynasty, it was referred to in the *Liji* (礼记) "Records of Rites." The Six Confucian Classics are regarded as the source of ancient Chinese scholarship and the foundation of traditional Chinese culture and social ideas.

fifty-two, he worked as Prime Minister in the Ministry of Justice. Following a disagreement among the powerful families, Confucius left his position and travelled around many other states, hoping he might have a chance to enact his political agenda. However, no rulers provided him with a position. In his later years, he went back to the state of Lu, continued his educational career, and taught nearly three thousand disciples in total, seventy-two of whom became noteworthy in their own right. Confucius rearranged the documents of poems, history, rituals and music inherited from Zhou Dynasty. These documents later became classics and the dominant teachings for traditional political education in China.

At the turning point of the Spring and Autumn Period and the Warring States Period (476-221 BC), radical transformation occurred economically, politically and socially. Throughout the prolonged societal chaos and conflict, the cultural tradition inherited from ancient times was corrupted. Being aware of this, Confucius carried on the mission of sustainment and resurrection of the great cultural tradition. The *Analects* is a collection of Confucius' words and deeds by his disciples and their followers. We can understand Confucius' political philosophy through the *Analects*.

Not only does Confucius exhibit keen observation of human affairs, but also a deep understanding of the movement of nature. Once Confucius stood over a riverbank and observed, "Isn't life's passing just like this, never ceasing day or night!" Confucius sighed over the passing water because he felt that existence flows continuously, just as Heraclitus (540-480 BC) considered everything in constant flux and movement, claiming we cannot step twice into the same river. Confucius noticed that *tian* does not speak, but the four seasons turn and the myriad things flourish. This is his illumination over natural creativity. However, Confucius does not discuss *tian* in detail, not in deduction,

Garden of stone inscription of the *Analects*. The garden was 300m south of the Confucian temple in Qufu, Shangdong Province. In this garden, the content of the *Analects* was written and carved on the stone walls.

An inscription in the stone garden.

nor even description. His method is vastly different from Western philosophical argumentation. However, both Chinese and Western philosophers share similar consciousness of philosophical concern despite their differences in philosophical thinking.

Confucius pays close attention to human reality, and tries to avoid mystical questions. He once told his students that if one cannot understand life, why should one think much about death? He does not totally deny the existence of gods and spirits, but he was chiefly concerned with participants' spiritual presence in sacrificial ceremonies. He holds that one can respect the gods and spirits but should keep them at a distance, and should not go into the details of whether those gods and spirits really exist or not. Therefore, though Confucianism is not a religion in the strict sense, it functions as a kind of religion in the lives of Chinese people.

In the *Analects*, Confucius does not mention much about *tian* (nature). This indicates that Confucius is not concerned with nature as much as human affairs. He mostly discusses issues of political philosophy.

Confucianism is an uplifting philosophy full of sagacity and magnificence, both necessary components of a community cultivating its communal spirituality. Confucius was a great thinker who had a great understanding of the ancient ritual system and classics, though he himself did not write much. He taught his disciples ancient classics, passed them from one generation to another, and thus formed the Confucian School. In this way, Confucian spirituality began with the nobility of

Confucius' identity, combined with his life experience and concerns for his state and people. This so-called religion finally came to be an inextricable part of Chinese culture after the sustained efforts of many generations of Confucianists'.

The focus of Confucian teaching is the *dao* of culture, i.e., "this culture of ours (*siwen* 斯文)." Confucius called himself the successor of the flourishing culture of the Zhou Dynasty. He devoted himself to the *dao* of culture, thinking that a person devoted to cultural transmission is necessarily strong and resolved, for they bear a heavy charge and need to travel great lengths.

In one story, Confucius asked his four disciples to express their ideals. He does not praise the first three students, who only want to stick to his teachings and perform their duties. Instead he stresses one's own style to conduct and perform. Confucius agrees with the fourth student, Zeng Dian, who merely expressed his desire to accompany some young men and children over to the Yi River, where they will cleanse themselves, revel in cool breezes at the Rain Altar, and return home singing. From this story we see that Confucius not only cares for formal matters, but is also appreciative of many other joys. He stimulates his students to be inspiring, which exemplifies the ideal level of Confucian philosophy. Because Confucian philosophy uplifts the spirit in this way, it attracted much attention at various points in history, making it a part of mainstream Chinese culture.

In Confucian thought, the most fundamental relationship is between father and son. After a person is born into this world, it is impossible for one to change

The Classic of Filial Piety

The Classic of Filial Piety is a classic Confucian treatise giving advice on filial piety. It was composed sometime between the Qin and Han dynasties, with some scholars attributing it to Confucius. The book deals with the sole subject of filial piety, holding that filial piety is a sign of natural law, a behavioral standard for human beings and the foundation of national politics. It is what a ruler bases his or her state governing principles and what the people follow to behave and manage their families. *The Classic of Filial Piety* makes an overall explanation of the exact meaning of filial piety, helping people get a deeper understanding of filial piety, advising them to cherish their lives and to coordinate between themselves and their living environment, so as to rule the country with filial piety. *The Classic of Filial Piety* was honored as a Confucian classic in the Tang Dynasty and listed as one of the Thirteen Classics after the Southern Song Dynasty. The moral principles stated in *The Classic of Filial Piety* have become part of the key components of traditional Chinese ideas.

Confucius and his disciples.

his or her birth place, parents or other family relationships. Since these relationships are inevitable, the Confucian attitude is to comprehend them from their beginning and cultivate one's behavior into family reverence (*xiao* 孝).

In the *Analects*, family reverence is taken as the root of human feelings, a deep appreciation toward the original state of one's life. By enhancing one's primary familial relationships, a person enhances his or her family reverence. Humane love starts from close intimate feelings and extends to other people as one begins to love holistically. Family reverence is the root of humaneness. If people concentrate their efforts on the root, the way (*dao*) will grow therefrom. A human's feelings start with reverence towards family, and spread over all of humanity.

Confucius extends his thoughts on family reverence to social management, and infuses his governing principle with morality and ritual propriety. For Confucius, law can prevent people from doing wrong things, but does not help them avoid shameful punishments. An exemplary person needs to cultivate others with morality, and guide their rituals. After people develop a sense of moral justice, they can bring order to their lives.

In short, Confucius thinks that a human being can only fulfill him or herself by beginning with family reverence, the starting point of all relationships. We must be aware of this innate feeling so we can nourish and cultivate it, and extend it to other social relationships, such as ruler-minister, husband-wife, and friendship. In this way, Confucius founded a theory of cultivating one's behavior toward family and society, which aims to establish harmonious relationships by recovering their origin.

The central theme of Confucius' thought is "humanity" (ren仁) which is composed of the characters "two" (er 二) and "human" (ren 人). Originally, "ren" shared other meanings as "ren" (妊), which means to be pregnant. Etymologically, this latter character denotes a mother being linked with her baby. Thus, "ren" originally refers to the parental feelings between a mother and her baby. The later meaning of *ren* is an extension of love. It may have been conceived that the origin of human relationships is the basic human feelings between mother and child. At the moment the umbilical cord of a mother is cut, the primordial relationship between mother and baby transforms to be a post-heaven intimate relationship, and the bodily link between blood and flesh becomes a relationship of intimate feelings. This original feeling is what later extends to different social relationships. Centered only on humanity, Confucius' thought is not entirely concrete. Mencius later developed "ren" into a systematic political philosophy, extending the meaning from an individual person to a moral view of the world.

In the *Analects*, the process of developing humaneness (*ren*) is mainly conducted through ritual propriety (*li*). Confucius stresses many times that only with sincere humane love can ritual propriety have real significance. In human communication, the most important factor is one's feelings toward others, while the form of this sentiment comes secondary. Thus, Confucius' comprehension and appreciation of the origin of human feelings is sharp and profound.

The exemplary person (*junzi*) mentioned in the *Analects* is a moral model or leader. Confucius claims that if a leader treats his family and friends well, others will follow his example. The virtue (*de*) of an exemplary person can influence that of the petty person just like wind can bend grass. He also mentions that when a person of excellent virtue takes a position of leadership, the multitude follow him respectfully like the North Star. Thus, the virtue of one can influence a whole nation.

Confucius' Platform in the Confucian Temple, Qufu, Shandong Province.

Ceremony of Worshipping Confucius in the Confucian Temple.

For one to realize humaneness, Confucius brings up the method of "disciplining the self and observing ritual propriety (*keji fuli* 克己复礼)." A person should realize that one's selfish desire might affect others negatively, and disobeys the requirement that ritual propriety demands. "If for the span of a day one were able to accomplish this, the whole world would defer to this humane model." This means that being humane is not an impossible goal. If one wants to reach it, one will get there. One can arrive at the realm of humaneness simply if one's ideas toward others are cultivated properly and steadily. "Becoming humane in one's conduct is self-originating - how could it originate from others?" Confucius thinks that everybody should be able to become humane, since it is simply an idea all can achieve.

Ren is realized thus: if you want to establish yourself, establish others; if you want to live free and easy, let others live free and easy. In handling the relationships, one should promote others when promoting oneself. If one does not want to be treated in a certain way, then do not treat others in that way. If one understands that everyone shares the same mind, and all minds share the same patterns, you should not treat people in the way you do not want to be treated.

In order to fulfill the political ideal of *ren*, Confucius brings forth ritual (*li* 礼) to put "humanity" (ren) into practice and make it a reality. However, he only presents the operating principle for *li*, which was not well developed until Mencius established his political system.

Mencius (Mengzi): Governing the State with Humane Love

Mencius (Mengzi, 372-289 BC) was from the state of Zou, in the present Zou County of Shandong Province. His father died when he was young. It was his mother's teachings that changed his life.

Many stories are told of how his mother educated him to be a great scholar. She moved home three times to better his upbringing. They first lived close to a graveyard, where young Mencius learned the rituals of the burial ceremony. His mother felt this was not good for his mental health, so she moved to a market. But there she soon found the young scholar imitating market behavior, so she moved to live near a school. She finally felt comfortable and resided there when she saw Mencius learning ritual ceremony by playing games with other children.

The story of Mencius' mother moving her home indicates that people are easily influenced by their environment. It also underlines the fact that human beings as active agents have the power to choose the place they want to live. This is part of the Confucian creed that cultivating oneself means cultivating your body's

Mencius

co-existence with your living environment. From the perspective of Mencius' mother, if she could help young Mencius choose a better environment, she would be able to help him live a better life, and he would thus be more likely to make better choices throughout his life.

Mencius studied Confucius' philosophy and promoted it. Like Confucius, he travelled to many states wanting to persuade rulers to adopt his doctrines. He travelled more extravagantly than Confucius, with many chariots and followers. However, just as most rulers denied Confucius, Mencius' advice was also not welcome. His words seemed irrelevant to political matters. In his later years, Mencius went back home and taught several disciples (such as Wang Zhang), and wrote the book of *Mencius*, which earned him the title "Second Confucius" in Chinese cultural history.

Mencius remained strongly idealistic throughout his life. We

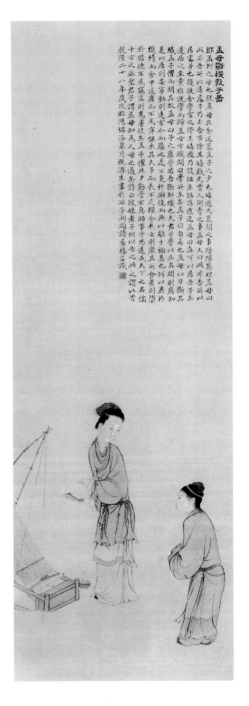

Mencius' mother cutting the thread of her loom to educate Mencius, King Tao, Qing Dynasty. Mencius' mother cut through her thread to show her son that neglecting his learning was just like her destroying her weaving.

might say that Mencius is a book full of moral idealism, or moral metaphysics, which puts morality over metaphysical thinking. The mind of his moral metaphysics refers not to the mind in its universal, simple, individual sense, but to a mind that is able to penetrate through the myriad things in the universe. Mencius' mind is not the mind of knowing with simple direction, but a mind that conceives of the transformation of things and events in the cosmos.

Mencius liked to debate forcefully, and he did not take rulers in power very seriously. He thought that mundane rulers only own their status, fame and power in the real world. He considered himself to be equal to them based on his assumption that he owned "heavenly honors" gifted from *tian*, i.e., the inborn heart-mind, nature, humane love and appropriateness, which are enough to parallel the status and achievements of all rulers. Mencius was very confident and insisted on reading books with independent thought. He contended that if one believes all that is written in historical books, it might be better that such books never existed. Thus, a true scholar ought never to be credulous in evaluating words or texts.

In the traditional system of Chinese monarchy, the leader is the center of the state. But as Mencius wanted to enlighten the benighted, he deviated from the norm. He even asserts that people are more valuable than rulers. He advocates a "well-field system," letting farmers have their private land with reduced taxes. To him, the lower class will be stable in mind only after they have stable property. He also condones a division of social labor, claiming that people who use their minds should rule others, while people who use their body should be ruled.

Mencius' answer to the ethical dilemma is full of idealism. Such is the widely debated issue about relatives hiding one another. The father of sage King Shun was a notoriously evil man. A student of Mencius once raised this question: if Shun's father killed someone, and Gao Yao, famous for his integrity, was the Minister of Justice, what would Shun do? Mencius answered that Shun's father would have to be captured because Shun would need to rule the state with legal regulations, so he would not prevent Gao Yao from capturing his own father. However, Mencius continued that because Shun is so filial, he would resign from the position of emperor to support his father, and enjoy living with him in peace on a remote seashore. Whether or not Mencius' plan is feasible, he emphasizes that one's intimate feelings toward one's father should be far more important than public opinion. To some extent, this family reverence should be prioritized over legal regulations. This assumption has led to many debates asking whether intimate feelings or legal regulations are more important.

Some criticize Mencius' implication that feelings take precedence over law, arguing that this prioritization has imbued corruption in Chinese society throughout history. But some disagree with this view, remarking that if Shun does place intimate feelings far above legality, his sentiment will deter Gao Yao from capturing his father. He might even threaten Gao Yao to resign or punish him. Yet it is clear that Mencius promotes the rationality of ruling the state by law, and so Shun would not interfere if Gao Yao were to punish his father according to the law.

Nevertheless, in the later part of the scenario when Shun's father is captured, Shun wishes to maintain his family reverence to his father by giving up the highest position. This is related to the relationship between family and state, intimate feelings and justice. For Mencius, the state is not as important as family, and social justice is not as important as close relationships. When these are in opposition, we should give up the state to preserve family because the integrity of one's family is the foundation for the unity of a state. Also, by the same token, personal intimate feelings should be valued over communal justice.

In regard to this ethical dilemma, debaters justify, gloss over, or even radically attack traditional Confucian relationships as the foundation for social corruption. But the scenario is not quite an accurate depiction of ancient Chinese society. The real dilemma would most likely have fallen on Gao Yao himself, not on the ruler, Shun. Usually a minister would think over the dilemma that his emperor faced, and try his best to solve the impasse on his own. Because it would bring shame and difficulty upon the emperor if his father was captured, the minister may concede to avoid such a scenario. Yet if he does not capture the emperor's father, he is not a competent judge who upholds the law. Clearly Gao Yao would have difficulty reconciling his dilemma between loyalty and justice. This is a typical illustration of the ethical conflict between loyalty (*zhong* 忠) and appropriateness (*yi* 义) in ancient Chinese society. It also demonstrates the struggle of actualizing humane love as prescribed by Mencius' doctrine.

In order to demonstrate the real possibility of governing by humane love, Mencius proposes his views on the heart-mind and human nature.

Once King Xuan of Qi saw an ox trembling before it was sent to be sacrificed. He felt it was miserable and ordered it be replaced by a sheep. Mencius told the king that if the king has some feelings of condolences towards a dying ox, he should extend it to his people. The ruler's unbarred mind can be expressed through loving people and taking measures whereby people might also enjoy his pleasure.

For Mencius, the unbarring mind reflects on the fundamental concerns of living existence. He takes this as the starting point of human nature. It is a feeling of condolence over other's sufferings and the knowledge that oneself might face the same kind of suffering. Its foundation is the continuity of bodily existence and the sharing of similar feelings towards life and suffering. The feeling of commiseration is an extension of

The Mencius Temple, also called "The Second Confucius Temple," in Zoucheng, Shandong.

Confucian family reverence and brotherhood. Knowledge of family reverence is derived from sentiment toward parents, and brotherhood extends family reverence to one's siblings. Mencius enriches the Confucian sense of intimate feelings. Mencius' idea of commiseration is derived from the assumption that others may face similar sufferings. Thus, deep condolences for natural suffering result from empathy toward any human being or animal. Compared to Confucius' optimism that human feeling can flourish from family reverence to brotherhood, trustworthiness, loyalty and humane love, Mencius is more concerned with bemoaning the state of the universe and pitying the fate of human beings. Mencius admits that misfortune is mankind's destiny, but shows dedication to human emotion, as well as deep concern for worldly affairs and human suffering.

Mencius divides the Confucian original state of family reverence into four parts, which he calls "the four moral sprouts" (*siduan* 四端): the feeling of commiseration, the awareness of shame and distaste, the sentiment of modesty and yielding, and the sense of right and wrong. He thinks that these four beginnings are the basic points of human nature. They are inherent in human beings, and can develop into diverse human feelings: humane love (*ren* 仁), appropriateness (*yi* 义), ritual propriety (*li* 礼) and wisdom (*zhi* 智).

For Mencius, human beings naturally have sympathy for the weak and helpless, i.e., feelings of commiseration toward the suffering of others. At the moment one sees a child ready to fall into a deep well, one is bound to feel anxiety in one's heart, and will naturally run to save it. Every person is inclined to save the child because every person shares a certain sense of sympathy. Mencius takes these feelings of commiseration to be the motivator of good deeds. These feelings can develop into sympathy, understanding and care for others. In short, the good heart-mind originates in one's natural feeling of commiseration. This is the moral foundation for everyone.

Mencius' thought experiment of a child falling into a well is a rather extreme circumstance. Mencius illustrates it in this way to display, through experiment, a natural human intuition. In extreme cases, a particular action may not be necessary. Saving a child from falling lacks any necessary utilitarian motive. Befriending its parents or seeking praise are certainly not selfless motives. But if human beings can possibly help others without any consideration for their own well-being, it seems there lies an inherent goodness in the heart-mind of every human.

As for the other three "moral sprouts," the awareness of shame and distaste means humans were born with a sense of shame, which is a kind of self-consciousness of misdoings. The sentiment of modesty and yielding is the inborn understanding of ritual propriety, illustrating the proper guidelines for speech or action. The sense of right and wrong is not only moral, but also a judgment towards human affairs, so it can be taken as evidence of an epistemological mind.

Mencius holds that the four sprouts are the basis for the existence of human beings. Among them, the feeling of commiseration is prior to one's sense of right and wrong. This means that Mencius emphasizes feeling over knowing. This also proves that the core of his philosophy is governance by humane love, not an understanding of the world itself.

Mencius stresses reflection as a method for maintaining one's natural good heart-mind. Human beings usually do not realize the importance of holding onto one's own good heart-mind, just as they may carelessly lose a hen or dog. For this reason, Mencius promotes efforts to "find one's lost mind." Through a continuous effort of cultivation, one can be fulfilled with great morale (*haoranzhiqi*) that "is to be above the power of riches and honors to make dissipated, of poverty and mean condition to make swerve from principle, and of power and force to make bend - these characteristics constitute the great man." Mencius stresses the method of cultivating great morale because he faces the dilemma of putting his political philosophy of governing by humane love into practice. In order for his governing ideal to be justified, he must place the value of morality over achievements in human affairs. His method of inner-rectitude had a strong impact on Confucianists, especially those who were frustrated in handling human affairs.

Laozi: The Great *Dao* is like Water

Laozi lived at roughly the same time as Confucius. It was said that Confucius once consulted Laozi, and respected him very much, saying, "Isn't Laozi just like a dragon!" Laozi was once the head of the national library of the Zhou Dynasty. He was both a great scholar and a recluse. Upon discovering the corruption of politics, he decided to retire, travelling west on the back of an ox. The gatekeeper of the western border supposedly saw purple *qi*

Laozi travelling west on the back on an ox.

in the east, and was able to guess that Laozi was coming. He kept Laozi at the gate and asked him to transcribe his philosophy. This is the legend of the *Daodejing*, a Daoist classic roughly 5,000 words long.

Like Confucius, Laozi brings forward a systematic political philosophy. He argues further on the source of *dao*. His idea of *dao* succeeds the *dao* in *Zhouyi* that penetrates through heaven and earth and human affairs.

While *The Book of Changes* explores the *dao* of *tian* for the purpose of understanding human affairs, the *Daodejing* explores the *dao* of water for the purpose of understanding personal events. *Laozi* draws many important conclusions based on his understanding of water, both subtly and powerfully. Confucius once signed over the passing water, and Laozi similarly declared that the highest good in the world is like water, for it benefits everything without struggle. Since water dwells in places avoided by most, its way is similar to *dao*. The basic form of *dao* is like the ceaseless spring under the earth. The *dao* of heaven and earth forever produces things and events and destroys them.

The cosmological *dao* of the myriad things is like a great fetal beginning, out of which everything flows.

Dao is the road on which people walk, and the words people say. It can be comprehended as the pattern human beings use to communicate with the world. This pattern is close to the way beyond names and language - the original state of communication with the world. *Dao* is not a name, it is the way-making that humans travel, linking them to the world as soon as they begin to walk and talk. In both Ancient Chinese and Latin, a single word is used for both walking and talking. Hence, *dao* and the Latin "logos" are comparable in this sense.

The profundity of the *Daodejing* not only encourages people to examine their relationship with the world, but also to think through it. Laozi promotes the sensibility of being integrated with nature without a linguistic system or method of expression. Thus, Laozi puts forward a special way of "*dao*-talking-for him," whatever can be written down is not the *dao* itself. *Dao* is changing and moving, but is relatively constant. The same is the case for names. If you call something by a name, it is not that literal name. However, human beings have to use such linguistic and expressive systems to communicate with the world.

Laozi's thinking through opposition shows he is more profound than Confucius in some respects. Confucius taught people what they should do and how to do it, but Laozi taught in an opposite way of thinking and doing. Through his understanding of water, Laozi appreciates the power of being weak and yielding. Few understand the reason why the weak prevails over the strong, and act according to it. This does not mean that if one understands one aspect, the other is self-evident. Actually, neither aspect can exist independently from its opposite part. *Dao* always moves to its counter aspect and works through its weakening process. Water is soft and weak, but can be extremely destructive. Floods can be devastating, and the constant drip of water can wear holes in a stone. Water is powerful because it has incomparable tenacity.

It is *The Book of Changes* and the *Daodejing* that set the foundation for Chinese cosmological studies full of yin-yang interchanging and cyclical return. It can be argued that the ancient Chinese had a cyclical conception of time and space. Contrastingly, the Western philosophical view of time and space is linear.

Laozi wrote down these words, which might still be the obscurest of the obscure: "Way-making (*dao*) that can be put into words is not really way-making." It seems whatever he wrote is not dependable, and whatever is dependable is not constant way-making. Thus, one of the typical characteristics of *dao* is obscurity. This is perpetuated in the next line, "naming (*ming* 名) that can assign fixed references to things is not really naming. The nameless (*wuming* 无名) is the fetal beginnings of everything that is happening (*wanwu* 万物), while that which is named is their mother." This means

Laozi Lecturing, Ren Yi, Qing Dynasty.

that the more the *dao* is discussed, the further it is away from constancy.

The real *dao* is beyond description since once it is put into words, it is no longer fundamental, basic and lasting. Like the beginning of the cosmos, *dao* always creates, but we cannot depict it clearly, so we can only provide the name *dao* for it. *Dao* is a state that people can feel but cannot speak of.

Laozi uses two concepts: being (*you* 有) and non-being (*wu* 无) to support the idea that *dao* is beyond words. Existentially, "non-being" is a state of emptiness, the nothingness prior to the cosmos. Thus it is phrased as "*wu* (non-being)." It is often called "the fetal beginning of the myriad things" to admit that things must have begun at a state of being named (*youming* 有名). The question of whether being or non-being came first has been difficult to answer throughout the history of philosophy. The state of the original happening of heaven and earth is beyond words, so we can only use "being" and "non-being" to describe it. Thus, from an existential perspective, the meaning of being and non-being is restricted to something and nothing.

However, in an ontological sense, the words "you (being)" and "wu (non-being)" are used to discuss whether things and events generate from a state of "being" or "non-being." Laozi admits that exact nothingness could be the starting point of the world, but he feels it is necessary for the world to have a substantial beginning with form and image, just as a mother gives birth to a child. Laozi describes this as "the gateway of the dark female." However, there are many disputes over Laozi's idea of "nothingness (*wu*)." Various interpretations surround the discussion of whether the cosmic origin is "non-being (*wu*)" or "nameless (*wuming*)."

Being and non-being emerge from the same source yet are referred to differently. "Together they are called obscure. The obscurest of the obscure, they are the swinging gateway of the manifold mysteries." The theory that the heavens communicate with the earth makes it seem as though they emerge from the same source. Viewed from this perspective, "being" and "non being" are just names. Viewed from another perspective, they seem to be different states. They are both ultimate states of existence, relative to one's perspective. Laozi shows us there are many ways to grasp the world, and these ancient philosophers' fundamental points of view lead us into their unique visions about the world.

For Laozi, the *dao* of heaven and earth is continuous with the *dao* of politics. The foundation of the *Daodejing* is rooted in Laozi's concern for the *dao* of ruling states and pacifying the chaos of the Spring and Autumn Period.

Laozi's political philosophy is purposefully designed for kings of states. Laozi thinks a king's character should imitate that of rivers and seas, as he writes, "what enables the rivers and seas to be king over all the valleys is that they are good at staying lower than them." Valleys are lower than streams, and rivers and seas are lower than valleys. This is the reason why rivers and seas can be confluent of hundreds of streams and valleys. Laozi draws conclusions from

The Guodian Chu Tomb Scripts.

natural phenomena to persuade those on top to be as humble as possible. The sages put themselves behind common people so as to maintain their positions, and though they cared not for themselves, they were always protected. Laozi finds that those who always prepare to fight with others get less than they wish, but those who do not fight with others get more than they have expected.

For Laozi, the character of a king is shown through actual achievements, though he should remain non-coercive in his endeavors. Laozi believes a huge state must be governed as one cooks a small fish, which will be burned and ruined if turned too often. Clearly, Laozi suggests a need for a gentle hand in governing. The more crafty rulers are, the craftier the ruled become. Therefore, if governing guidelines change often, people will be difficult to deal with. Laozi emphasizes that those in power should not interfere with the peaceful life of common people.

Laozi's ideal way of ruling is to keep the populace uninformed. Confucius shares a similar idea that people should be asked to do what they should, but there is no need to explain their purpose. Laozi insists on governing a state without promoting intelligence. He reasons that people will have good fortune if a leader looks foolish and handles affairs without guile. The best ruling pattern is not to let people know much, but to make sure they are healthy. Power comes from the proper state of non-coercive action, but few leaders practice reticence. Most of them witness the power of activity, but neglect the advantages of being non-assertive.

Laozi thinks that when grand way-making is abandoned, humaneness (ren) and appropriateness (yi) appear. It is when wisdom (zhi) and erudition arise that great duplicity appears. When the six family relationships are disharmonious, family reverence (xiao) and parental affection (ci) appear. When the states

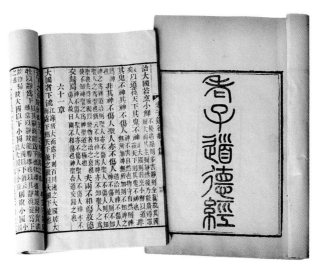

An ancient version of *Daodejing*.

have fallen into troubled times, upright ministers appear (Chapter 18). Confucianism advocates humanity (*ren*), appropriateness (*yi*), family reverence (*xiao*), and loyalty (*zhong*) which Laozi does not support. Laozi thinks that human beings emulate the earth, the earth emulates the heavens, the heavens emulate way-making, and way-making emulates what is spontaneously so (*ziran* 自然). Everything is self-perpetuating and the *dao* follows its pattern in itself.

Laozi's idea of "small states of few people" is to build an ideal society, where a leader is instructed thus: "Bring the common people back to keeping their records with knotted string, to relishing their food, to finding beauty in their garments, to enjoying their customs, and to finding security in their homes. Although your neighboring states are within eyesight, and the sounds of their dogs and cocks are within earshot, your people will grow old and die without having anything to do with them." This is a summary of Laozi's ideal society. His idea of "small states of few people" brings ultimate expectations and imagination to those in crowded cities today.

Laozi argues that "to know others is wisdom; to know oneself is acuity (*ming*)." Those who are enlightened understand themselves the most, so they know what to do and what not to do. Self-discovery is achieved through the understanding of how things work and develop, i.e., the *dao* of movements. A person who is illuminated is able to immerse and participate in events and lead their changing process. One who lacks acuity and tries to do things without control will create disaster. Thus, to have acuity (*ming*) is to tread the desirable path on the middle ground

English translation of *Daodejing*.

between extremes. This is attained from deep appreciation of the living experience. Personal growth and development consists of learning the changes of events, which in turn grants the observer a deeper understanding of him or herself. Thus, acuity is an understanding of the relationship between the self and others.

Laozi also points out that "to conquer others is power, to conquer oneself is strength." A human being's communication with the world is subtle and delicate. If one has difficulty in achieving something, it may be because his or her rhythm does not resonate with his or her surroundings. Usually people need to work hard and suffer from their experience so they can achieve a harmonious rhythm with the world and prevail.

For Laozi, sages have a delicate and accurate intelligence to understand mystical things, and need not venture beyond their doors to know what is going on in the world. The central doctrine

French version of *Daodejing*.

of Laozi's epistemology is intuitive enlightenment. One's fundamental enlightenment about the world relies on intuition concerning the original existence of things. Enlightening through intuition is a typical method of Chinese epistemology. It can be argued that intelligence and intuition play much more important roles than experience or logical deduction in Laozi's epistemology. How can one keep one's intuitive sensibility in the process of acquiring scientific knowledge? It seems very difficult, but Laozi insists that we need to cultivate acute intuition based on our experience of the world.

It seems Laozi counters common sense in saying, "in studying, there is a daily increase; in learning of way-making (*dao*), there is a daily decrease." This implies that the more knowledge one has, the less *dao* and intuition one uses for things and events. Here what Laozi emphasizes is a process of diminishing in learning *dao*, which encourages his "non-coercive acting." Laozi's non-coercive doing conquers the whole world by "going about business without interfering," which is not just for a king ruling the world, but for everyone who can comprehend the world in totality. "By interfering, you make yourself unworthy of ruling the world." The world can only be holistically realized through non-interfering. The more one does for the world, the further one drifts from it. One needs to be contextualized in the world, following its changes. Thus, one might have control over the world though it seems they do not interfere with it at all.

Zhuangzi: Wandering at ease without Self

Zhuangzi (c. 369-286 BC) lived in the state of Song on the border of present Shandong and Henan Province. In his early life he made a living by weaving straw sandals, and later he became a small officer in charge a garden of sumac, living a meagre lifestyle. Today the book of *Zhuangzi* has seven Inner Chapters, fifteen Outer Chapters, and eleven Miscellaneous Chapters. Zhuangzi employs every resource of rhetoric in his writings and persuades people to free themselves from societal bondage, which is exactly the opposite of Confucian teachings. For a Confucian, it is important to be involved in the world, but Zhuangzi challenges people to be free from its shackles. It can be argued that Zhuangzi's political philosophy focuses on the limitations of one's body and the settlement of one's mind.

Zhuangzi uses fables to convey the limits of politics. In order to help people deal with the shackles of power, he encourages them to free themselves and wander in a free and easy way. Zhuangzi recognizes that people are confined in the "rivers and lakes" which are metaphors for the social system and structure of power. Humans live their lives entrenched in various social relationships, so it is very difficult for them to be freed. In his first chapter "Free and Easy Wandering," Zhuangzi proposes wandering as the key point to his philosophy. Of course he admits that it is extremely difficult to be free in the world of power, so he provides an illustration of "no-self." The *Zhuangzi* is a book that teaches people to not take themselves too seriously so they may extricate themselves from the struggle of power.

When Zhuangzi's wife died, his good friend Hui Shi went to console him, only to find Zhuangzi sitting on the ground, singing. Hui Shi asked Zhuangzi how he could be so unkind to his wife. Zhuangzi said that when his wife had just died, he

Zhuangzi

could not help feeling sorrow. Soon, however, he thought over the whole matter and realized that she was not living, having no form, nor even breath. She seemed to live between being and non-being. Somehow or other she transformed from *qi* to form, then to life. When she died, she went back from life to *qi*. What Zhuangzi wants to argue is that if one takes the life process as a transformation of *qi*, one will not attach so much affection to it. From Zhuangzi's perspective, human beings come from the natural *qi* just like all the myriad things, *qi* transforms to form, and the form travels the world. The life process from birth to death is like the change of the four seasons. Zhuangzi advocates an attitude of freedom, proposing that human beings follow natural rhythm and be harmonious with it since human beings are also part of nature.

Zhuangzi was a hermit who lived a poor but peaceful life. When King Wei of Chu heard Zhuangzi was available, he sent two officers with lots of money to inaugurate him as Prime Minister for the state. Zhuangzi was busy fishing, and without turning his head, he told them a story: "I have heard that there is a sacred tortoise in Chu that has been dead for three thousand years. The King keeps it wrapped in cloth and boxed, and stores it in the ancestral temple. Now would this tortoise rather be dead and have its bones left behind and honored? Or would it rather be alive and dragging its tail in the mud?" Zhuangzi would rather enjoy himself in the mud. It was clear that Zhuangzi only wanted to fish, not to gain more power. High position and a good salary could not inspire Zhuangzi to leave his free and easy life of wandering. He believes a real hermit is one who keeps his mind detached. For Zhuangzi, a free and easy wandering existence is much more important than power, and so people can choose to reject it.

Zhuangzi realizes that humans are most confined by the unavoidable presence of body. Thus, Zhuangzi brings forth his ontology of making things equal and "living without self" as his method of being free from real political structure.

For Zhuangzi, the distinctions among things are relative. From the perspective of *dao*, there is no real difference or demarcation among things. All differences are perceived from man's diverse perspectives. Things have no difference or nobility or base from the perspective of *dao*, but they all consider themselves to be noble and others base from their own perspectives. Thus, being and non-being, true and false are all determined by human perspectives. Zhuangzi draws the conclusion that "the heavens and the earth live together with me" and "all things are continuous with me."

Zhuangzi and Hui Shi Debating over the River Hao, Li Tang, Song Dynasty.

Zhuangzi points out that small birds cannot understand the height or distance a huge seabird can fly. Things have different inner natures, and the relativity of things and events are what the world is composed of. If one admits a natural difference among things and events, and they are all self-fulfilled in their own natures, there would be no distinctions among things. Things have their own natural ways of transforming, and people should not force their intentions onto other things and events. He deems it unwise to put a halter around a horse's neck or a string through an ox's nose because these are contrary to the natures of these animals.

In "The Secret of Caring for Life," there is a story about "Cook Ding cutting an ox." Cook Ding had used his knife for nearly nineteen years, and the knife was still like new. His explanation was that he knew the structure of an ox's body, so when his knife entered the ox's body, the knife transformed into its edge, so it was like entering a world of nothingness. The metaphor behind this story is that society is like the complex body of an ox, and a human being goes through it like a knife. A knife needs to be transformed into its edge so it can wander freely in the body of an ox. Turning a knife into its edge is analogous to nullifying one's body. For Zhuangzi, one should not take one's body as concrete as it seems to be. If one takes oneself as the knife and not its edge, then one puts oneself in a position equal to other materials and will hurt oneself in the end. The way to wander free and easy is to transform oneself to have no form, and to exist as if there is no self. Thus can one be free like the edge of a knife in a structure of power. This is the way that Zhuangzi understands the human relationship with the world.

Zhuangzi thinks great benefits may come from seemingly useless things. For example, he realizes that the most beautiful trees are the first to be killed by a lumberjack. These trees do not live as long as they can. However, ugly-looking trees are seen

Zhuangzi dreaming of becoming a butterfly.

as useless to the lumberjack, and so they are often neglected. Their ugly appearance protects them from harm so they may live as long as possible. This is the advantage of being useless. Yet Zhuangzi also notices that a loud goose is liable to live longer, so he advocates a middle way between usefulness and uselessness.

For Zhuangzi, the reason big seabirds can fly high is because they rely on something else. Both look free, but they are actually not. Real freedom is "no reliance" (*wudai* 无待), i.e., totally depending on oneself and nothing else. The way to realize "no reliance" is to totally forget everything, which he calls "quiet sitting and forgetting" (*zuowang* 坐忘). In this state, one forgets the body and its sense organs, reaching a state of no self or mind, a state completely cognizant of what is happening. In this way,

Six Daoists at the Bamboo Stream by the modern painter Zhang Daqian. Among them is Li Bai, the greatest poet of the Tang Dynasty.

Zhuangzi thinks people can avoid the disturbance of ordinary affairs and remain invincible.

In "Fit for Emperors and Kings," Zhuangzi tells that when Hundun (Chaos) does not have seven openings it can sustain itself. But when it has seven openings to see, hear, eat and breathe, its *qi* will scatter and it slowly dies. Zhuangzi uses this fable to express the primordial state in its original sense. This state is not sustained through sense organs, but is reached through mind and the intuitive enlightenment that penetrates to the great *dao*. Zhuangzi admits through the death of Hundun that there exists an original chaotic state similar to the state of knowing *dao* or the pre-heaven state of human beings. However, when a person enters the world and communicates with it, this original state begins a process of scattering. Thus, a person should try to maintain this originality that links them to all things and events.

Once Zhuangzi dreamed of becoming a happy butterfly. Suddenly he awoke drowsily, and wondered whether he was Zhuangzi who had dreamt of being butterfly or a butterfly dreaming of being Zhuangzi. This fable displays the transformative continuity between dreams and reality. The best state of communication man can maintain with the world is the continuity between external things and himself. It seems that this state of continuity is the original state of human beings. In the moment that humans communicate with the world, their self-consciousness has not developed to separate them from the world. The continuity of human beings and external things shows they have not separated from the world. For Zhuangzi, the best way of facing the vicissitudes of life is to understand them in a chaotic and continual manner.

Zhuangzi believes the governor of a state should follow the nature of his people, and influence them without words or even mind. He is against the application of human technique or mechanism in governing. According to Zhuangzi, a sage should rectify his own morality and promote it to his people to let them do their best on their own. This ideal state of governing compares one's mind to traveling in a world of emptiness. It contains no selfishness. The ten thousand things grow according to their natures and everything flourishes. Zhuangzi is against any method of human control. He advocates the state of being together with the transformation of things, and flowing with their natural rhythm, so as to impose perfect and harmonious governance upon the world.

Mozi and other Pre-Qin Thinkers

Most of the political philosophers in the Pre-Qin era devoted themselves to recovering and reconstructing social orders, as did Mozi (c. 475-395 BC) who was from the state of Lu and active in the state of Song. Mozi studied Confucian theories when he was young, and created his own school after finding himself unsatisfied with Confucian teachings. Mozi travelled around the states to promote his ideas as he grew up, hoping emperors might take his advice seriously in ruling their states. But most emperors did not adopt what he said, so he was never appointed to any position.

Mozi was a great scientist of his time. It was said he invented many weapons and machines. He once spent three years inventing a wooden eagle but it flew for only one day. He once successfully persuaded the King of Chu not to attack the state of Song. The "Mohists" (*mozhe*) were those who put Mozi's ideas into practice. They were mostly intellectuals from the lower class, and their leader was called "huge master (*juzi* 巨子)." There was a strict system of law practice that required its members to "enter fire or tread on sword blades, and even death would not cause them to turn on their heels."

Compared with the sense of nobility that Confucianism entails, the political philosophy of Mozi has a strong foundation for ordinary people who aspire to form an ideal society. Mozi denies the accountability of war completely, and takes "the condemnation of war" as a fundamental principle for Mohism. He argues that if you consider others' bodies as parts of your own body, then you come to perceive "attacking" as ruining others' existence. If one takes others' bodies to be the same as one's own, one will not go to war.

"Universal love (*jian'ai* 兼爱)" is the theoretical premise for Mozi's condemnation of war. "Universal love" is to love all people without

Moxi

discrimination, no matter how far apart they may be, or how emotionally close they are. Mozi says, "universally loving one another will mutually benefit one another; universally hating one another will mutually harm one another." Mozi believes everyone needs to love each other so that one takes other states, families and bodies as one's own. The thought of "universal love" is close to the Western idea of philanthropy, and is much more unselfish than Confucian love of humanity.

Mozi promotes the idea of the will of heaven (*tianzhi* 天志). He thinks heaven has will and judgment, and rulers are the sons of heaven. Heaven might punish them, so rulers should be cautious about behaviors that might intrigue praise or punishment from heaven. The fundamental will of heaven is universal love. His idea that heaven has a will indicates that heaven has its own judgment of human affairs. Humans should willingly act according to the will of heaven.

Since heaven (*tian*) has a will, rulers must obey what *tian* favors. *Tian* wishes for people to behave well and love each other. If they do not, *tian* will punish them by means of ghosts and spirits. Mozi not only admits the existence of spirits, but considers them to be cleverer than sages. This reminds rulers that they should remain in awe of gods and spirits more powerful than them.

In ruling a state, Mozi advocates two points: promoting the able (*shangxian* 尚贤) and agreeing with a superior (*shangtong* 尚同). To "promote the able" is to select those who have the ability to participate in state affairs. For Mozi, everyone should have a chance to participate in social management no matter what kind of background they have. He encouraged rulers to select talented individuals regardless of their qualifications.

Mozi holds that those who are selected through promotion must meet with their superiors after they enter a state management system and discover their common ground. To "agree with a superior" is to reach agreement in thought and

Mozi persuading the King of Chu not to attack the state of Song.

political centralization. From Mozi's perspective, it is necessary to regulate ideas and reach political centralization.

Mozi condemns music. He takes it to be a luxury of little value to most people. From his point of view, policy should not burden the common people. It should be implemented according to their basic needs. Mozi also recommends thriftiness with funerals and burying because he believes spending money on the dead depletes the fortunes of the living. For Mozi, the dead should not compete with the living for resources. Being modest with funerals and reducing the cost of burying avoids a waste of such resources. "Condemning music" and "being restrained in burial" are ideals of citizens as opposed to nobles' wasting money on music and lavish funerals. Mozi believes rulers should spend time and money on the common people.

Mozi has a methodology for realizing the world by three tests of a judgment: its basis, its verifiability, and its applicability. The first tests the will of heaven and spirits and the deeds of ancient sage-kings. The second verifies the judgment using the eyes and ears of the common people. And the third observes whether the judgment is beneficial to the country and its people. Mozi hopes the common people will benefit from his tests of judgment. This is a pragmatic understating of truth.

Xunzi's Political Theory

Xunzi (313-238 BC) was born in the state of Zhao during the later Warring States Period. He was once a professor in the Academy of Jixia, a great center of learning of that time, and was appointed the president of this academy for three terms. Later, Xunzi was the leader of Lanling County. Today we can learn his thoughts from the book bearing his name.

From Xunzi's perspective, human nature is evil because people were born to pursue their own interests: envy, love, music and

Xunzi.

beauty all lead to evil deeds such as struggling, fighting, offending and so on. All human virtues are acquired through training since they are all accomplishments and refinements brought about by culture. For Xunzi, human nature is the unwrought material of the original, and virtues are the outcomes of refining human nature. Humans have a natural tendency to eat when hungry, and wear clothing when cold. The ritual system rooted in family reverence is imposed upon one's natural tendencies after birth. It is not naturally developed from one's original nature. Xunzi also emphasizes the universality of human education, stating: "any man in the street can become a Yu, the traditional sage." Xunzi admits that sagehood can be achieved through learning.

Xunzi proposes ruling a state based on the guideline of "ritual outside and law inside," which is the most realistic and profound aspect of Xunzi's political philosophy. This guideline reveals the secret of ruling a state in ancient China. It was because of this practice that state leaders never promoted Xunzi's political philosophy, though it actually served as their practical theory. On the surface, nearly all leaders applied Confucian principles to rule the country. However, they actually adopted Xunzi's idea that "human nature is evil" in political practice, as constructing a law system was serious business. The Western use of natural law did not enter the Chinese political tradition. It may be argued that the ancient Chinese legal system is the artifice and art of dictatorship. The man-made legal system works only if the interest of rulers is to govern the populace.

Xunzi brings forth the idea of cultivating normal peoples' desires and considers natural human desires to be reasonable.

But because human nature is evil, society will become disordered when desires are not satisfied. Thus, it is necessary to regulate and cultivate human desire.

The classic implication of political struggle is that human nature is evil. Xunzi proposed a systematic political philosophy with strong operative and realistic meanings. Xunzi represents the theoretical tendency in pre-Qin political philosophical movements because he does not emphasize the art of rulership, fighting and war.

Han Fei's Art of Rulership

Han Fei (c. 280-233 BC) was born into a royal house of the state of Han, in present western Henan Province. Han Fei was a stutterer but an able writer. He and Li Si (died 208 BC) were both students of Xunzi. Now we can understand his thought through the work bearing his name. It was said that the first emperor of Qin, upon reading and enjoying Han Fei's works, launched an attack on the state of Han which sent Han Fei to the state of Qin.

But Han Fei was jailed through a political intrigue because Li Si, his former fellow student, was jealous of his talent and favor. Han Fei was forced to commit suicide by taking poison in prison.

Han Fei adopts Xunzi's idea that human nature is evil and thinks that everyone has "a mind of self-interest" that only calculates one's own interest in carrying out practice. Thus, Han Fei is against the Confucian method of ruling a state with humaneness, and advocates serious penal law and strong punishments. He becomes a great synthesizer of legalism based on

Han Fei.

Legalism

Legalism was one of the main philosophic currents during the Warring States Period. The trends that were later called Legalism have in common a focus on strengthening the political power of the ruler, of which law is only one part. The most important surviving texts from this tradition are the *Hanfeizi* and the *Book of Lord Shang*. In the Qin Dynasty the ideas of Shang Yang and Li Si were essential in building the strong government that eventually defeated its rivals. Legalism was a pragmatic political philosophy that did not address higher questions like the nature and purpose of life. The school's most famous proponent and contributor, Han Fei, believed that a ruler should use three tools to govern his subjects.

former legalists' thoughts on powerful propensity, legal regulation and the art of rulership.

The propensity for power comes from variation. There is also this propensity among different people because there is a positional difference among people and their powers. There is a completely different relationship between a ruler and those ruled. This unequal relationship is the origin of the propensity for power. Han Fei wanted rulers to be extremely aware of the propensity for power and try their best to sustain it. Han Fei adopts Shen Dao's (c. 395-315 BC) thought on the propensity for power and thinks the most important things for an emperor are his position and power. Just as a fish cannot leave water, a ruler should embrace law while maintaining power.

Han Fei adopts Shang Yang's (d. 338 BC) method of emphasizing the significance of legal regulation, and proposes that law should be as manifested as much as possible for common people. However, Han Fei's idea of legal regulation is dramatically different from the Western idea of natural law in that his legal regulation is not based on any eternal universal principle. For Han Fei, the legal system is a system of praising and punishing common people that functions in the interest of rulers.

The art of rulership (*shu*) is based on the propensity for power, and works only for the aim of maintaining this propensity. Han Fei adopts Shen Buhai's (d. 337 BC) view of stressing statecraft and argues that it should not be seen by anyone. For Han Fei, statecraft should be kept secret in a ruler's mind. Ministers and common people should not understand such thoughts. In this way, a ruler can secretly control ministers and force them to fear him because they never know his real intentions.

The fundamental reason for a political ruler to apply the propensity of power, legal regulation and art of rulership was to maintain power and position. Thus, Han Fei's philosophical thought can be taken as the mechanism and art for political struggles.

Sunzi's *Art of War*

Sun Wu was born in the state of Qi (in the area of present-day Shandong province) as a contemporary of Confucius (551-479 BC) at the end of Spring and Autumn Period. He fled with his family to the state of Wu when Qi was in chaos. He assisted He Lü (r. 514-496 BC), the King of Wu with Wu Zixu as a military commander and defeated the state of Chu several times. Sun Wu wrote *The Art of War* in thirteen chapters.

The guideline of the *Art of War* is actually a fundamental distaste for warfare. One must go to war only when there is no alternative. For Sunzi, war is a vital matter of state. It is the field on which life or death is determined and the road that leads to either survival or ruin, and so it must be examined with the great care. The leaders of a state should be extremely wary of war unless there are absolutely no alternatives. Even military victory is a defeat in the sense that it requires an expenditure of a state's manpower and resources. For Sunzi, the most important factor in solving the conflict between states is to attack strategies. "The best military policy is to attack strategies; the next to attack alliances; the next to attack soldiers; and the worst to assault walled cities." Thus, the

Master Sun Wu.

highest stage of the art of war is to force the enemy to give up its attack.

Once one goes to war, one must control the whole situation, to control others without being controlled by others. One must adapt to changing situations on the battlefield. This requires a sensitivity and adaptability with the intuitive ability of a genius. One wrong idea might lead to the death of many soldiers. A general needs to control the situation with absolute commanding power, and remain at ease in the transformation of a battlefield. The changing situation on a battlefield requires a commander to have strong control over himself. As a commander, one should not have any self-interest in mind. He should only respond to changing situations. In these situations, a great commander is able to take full advantage of the circumstances, and achieve his purpose. Hence, for a great commander to make the right decisions, he must have distinguished character, a peaceful mind, and extremely accurate judgment.

There are five criteria that determine the outcome of a war: the way, climate, terrain, command and regulation. To gauge the outcome of a war it is necessary to appraise the following situations: How consistent is the thinking of the people with their superiors? How is the climate or the rotation of the seasons? Are there some advantages concerning the terrain on our side? How do the commanders compare? Does regulation entail organizational effectiveness? One needs to judge the possibility of winning a war from many perspectives. These are called the "five criteria (wushi 五事)."

It is important to evaluate the situation on both sides, and analyze it in detail. It is crucial to have full preparation before entering a war. Whether one is able to win a war is determined by the circumstances and manner of preparation. Sunzi points out that "he who knows the enemy and himself will never in a hundred battles be at risk." One key method of knowing one's

Sunzi's *Art of War*, bamboo strips in the Han Tomb of Yinqueshan, Linyi, Shandong Province.

enemy is the employment of spies. Only through accurate intelligence can one have confident control over the battlefield.

The *Great Learning* (*Daxue*), *Focusing the Familiar* (*Zhongyong*) and the four chapters of *Guanzi* elaborate the topic of self-cultivation in pre-Qin political philosophy. The *Great Learning* was originally a chapter of the *Book of Rites* (*Liji*). It was said to be written by Master Zeng, a disciple of Confucius. "The great learning" is learning to be a "great man" (*daren* 大人), which now means "adult" in Chinese. It also has the connotation of cultivating oneself to become a "great man" (exemplary person/sage). Traditionally it was taken as learning how to achieve the state of "inner sage-outer king (*neisheng waiwang* 內ネ饌王)." In pre-Qin political philosophy, the heart-mind-body-family-state process of self-cultivation in *The Great Learning* provides a practical pattern for later Confucianists.

Unlike *Daxue*, the *Zhongyong* supplies an operative model for an individual to face one's fundamental existential situation. This foundation for concern and anxiety (*jieshen*) is reminiscent of Confucius' model of political education. Confucius does not discuss *tian* in detail, but *Zhongyong* provides the mandate of heaven as a foundation for Confucian political education. In the *Analects*, Confucius does not mention the *dao* of *tian*, nor does he deliver a strong ontological foundation for his political education. But *Zhongyong*, written by Zisi, Confucius' grandson, sets a rather stable foundation, which is the mandate of heaven (*tianming*) mirroring the pattern of Confucian political education.

In *Guanzi*, there are four chapters titled "mechanism of heart-mind" (*xinshu*, two chapters), "purifying heart-mind (*baixin*)" and "art of functioning inner mind (*neiye*)." These four chapters focus on being "unfilled, focused, pacified and temporized." They explain the art of functioning one's mind in order to enlighten and control the world. This is done by incorporating pre-Qin political philosophy into personal self-cultivation and the continuity of personal *qi*-cosmology into the *qi* of the whole universe.

Chinese Metaphysics:

Interpretations of the World from Han to Tang Dynasties

The peak of ancient Chinese metaphysics was reached in the cosmology of the Han Dynasty (206 BC-220 AD), ontology in the Wei-Jin dynasties (220-589 AD) and Buddhist metaphysics in the Sui (581-618) and Tang (618-907) dynasties. The major topic of Chinese metaphysics is the relationship between the cosmos and life. The main focus of Han Dynasty metaphysics was to interpret the cosmos from different perspectives.

Chinese Cosmology in the Han Dynasty

The Shared Cosmological Diagram of Confucianists and Fortune-Tellers

The philosophical spirit of *Zhouyi*, "clarifying human affairs by understanding the *dao* of *tian*," was widely accepted as common sense. It was natural to consider the *dao* of *tian* as human affairs were mutually efficacious in the Han Dynasty. The Yin-Yang school constructed a systematic view of the cosmos in the pre-Qin era, and it was combined with the school of image-number in Zhouyi studies in the Han Dynasty, forming an extremely complicated system of image-number diagrams. This was mainly constructed with the concepts of yin and yang, corresponding exactly with five processes, four directions, four seasons, five tones, twelve months, twelve rhythms, ten Heavenly Stems, and twelve Earthly Branches. The school of Yin-Yang and the Five Processes were first applied to interpret the changes of myriad things in the cosmos, and then adopted widely into different disciplines, such as the calendar, music, medicine and mathematics, serving as the foundation for ancient Chinese science. The image-number diagram based on Yin-Yang and the Five Processes served as the scientific foundation for the actual lives of ancient Chinese people.

Han Dynasty cosmology evolved with the theories of the Yin-Yang school concerning natural disasters. For them, the cosmological model is discussed for fortune-telling in human affairs. Dong Zhongshu, Meng Xi, Jing Fang and the *Apocryphal Treatise on the Book of Changes* (*Yiwei* 易纬) all partook in this study. Dong described *tian* with a human face, and combined Yin-Yang thought with political philosophy in the Gongyang commentaries of the *Spring and Autumn Annals*. Meng Xi and Jing Fang developed image-number schools into different branches, such as tri/hexagrams and cosmological *qi*, eight directions, corresponding heavenly stems, changing tri/ hexagrams, and developed these schools into their mature forms. *The Apocryphal Treatise on the Book of Changes* (*Yiwei*) extended the image-number theory of tri/hexagrams to the interpretation of human affairs.

In the later era of the Western Han Dynasty (206 BC-25 AD), prophecy and apocrypha (*chenwei*) were very popular. The prophecies consisted of strange fortune-telling, and the apocrypha interpreted the Classics in great detail. *The Apocryphal Treatise on the Book of Changes* (*Yiwei*) discusses several stages of cosmological evolution: Great Nothingness (*taiyi*) during which the *qi* of cosmos has not dissipated; Great Origin (*taichu*) of *qi*; Great Beginning (*taishi*) of images; and Great Matter (*taisu*) of cosmological evolution. All these four stages are just one *qi*, when matter and *qi* have not yet been separated. The *Apocrypha* (*wei*) made Confucian classics religious, and interpreted the king and sage mystically to be immortals that transcend this world. *The Apocrypha of the Book of History* (*shangshu wei*), for example, regarded *The Book of History* as an authority for heaven and mystical sensibility. Confucius is described in the *Apocrypha of Spring and Autumn Annals* as mystically as possible.

Dong Zhongshu's Personification of *Tian* as Man's Great-Grandfather

In the Han Dynasty, the traditional study of Confucian classics was constructed, and it can be divided into an Old Text School and a New Text School, which indicate two methods of interpreting the ancient *Six Classics* (*liujing* 六经). The New Text School was written in the writing forms of the Han Dynasty, and focused on the meaning of reality. Dong Zhongshu's (179-104 BC) promotion of the Gongyang interpretation of the *Spring and Autumn Annals* (*chunqiu* 春秋) made this popular.

Dong Zhongshu

After establishing the Han Dynasty, the first emperor, Liu Bang, wanted to release people from years of war suffering, so he adopted his consultants' advice to put the Yellow Emperor-Laozi (*huanglao* 黄老) theory into practice, letting people rest for decades. The Han Empire became very wealthy during the time of Emperor Wu (r. 140-87 BC).

Dong Zhongshu was an excellent scholar of the *Spring and Autumn Annals* when he was young. He spent years on the *Gongyang Commentaries of the Annals* and combined political philosophy of the *Spring and Autumn Annals* with the Yin-Yang and Five Processes schools to form his own system of thinking.

Upon the succession of Emperor Wu, Dong persuaded him with theories of Yin-Yang and the Five Processes. Hence, his *Three Recommendations on Heaven and Human Beings* (*tianren sance* 天人三策) were accepted and transformed to be state policy. This made Confucianism the dominant study and wiped out the other hundred schools. Dong proposed the principle of Great Unification (*dayitong*) based on the *Spring and Autumn Annals* and the resonance between heaven and human beings. His philosophy can be found in his *Luxuriant Gems of the Spring and Autumn Annals* (*chunqiu fanlu* 春秋繁露).

Dong Zhongshu provides heaven with a human face and considers it the great-grandfather of mankind. In this way, the continuity of heaven and human beings is colored with an intimate sensibility, and the changes of the *dao* of *tian* are closely correlated with those of human affairs.

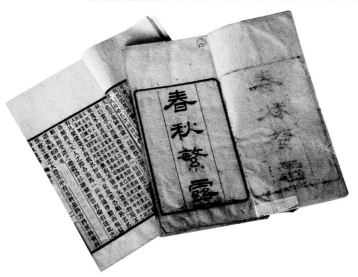

Dong Zhingshu's *Commentaries on the Spring and Autumn Annals.*

For Dong, *tian* is the operator of the myriad things it creates. Human beings are created according to the "heavenly numbers (*tianshu* 天数)" and a duplicate of heaven and earth. The structure of a human body is designed according to the model of *tian* in the following way: *tian* has 360 days, equal to the body's number of bones; *tian* has five processes, equal to the number of organs; *tian* has four seasons, equal to the number of limbs; *tian* has day and night, much like sleep and waking; *tian* has warm and cold, as we have favor and disfavor; *tian* has summer and winter, as we have happiness and anger. In short, Dong gives *tian* a human face in his theory, though he takes the human being to be a creation of *tian*.

Dong developed the thought of resonance between similar things to mean that *tian* and human beings must resonate with one another (*tianren ganying* 天人感应). He proposes a theory of "heavenly condemnation (*qiangao* 谴告)" explaining that *tian* would send down disasters as signals to alert rulers whenever the society is chaotic. Thus, *tian* is not only given a human face, but a relationship with humans suggesting that humans must follow the will of *tian*.

Dong was nearly beheaded for promoting the resonance between *tian* and human beings. In the year 135 BC, two royal houses of the Sacrifice Palace for imperial ancestors burst into flames, and Dong took it to be *tian's* anger toward Emperor Wu. His stance on this issue was heard by Zhufu Yan and presented to Emperor Wu, who was extremely angry and wanted Dong beheaded. It was Lü Bushu, Dong's disciple who pleaded for the emperor to spare Dong's life and remove his titles.

Later, Dong was appointed as prime minister for King Jiaoxi for several years. He retired to his hometown and wrote his *Commentaries on the Spring and Autumn Annals* in 121 BC. After Dong's death, Emperor Wu showed his compliments to Dong by dismounting when he passed by his tomb, thus Dong's tomb is also called "tomb of dismounting." This was a poignant moment in Chinese intellectual history, when an emperor paid respects to a particular scholar.

Baihutong's Correlation of Cosmology and Ethics

In the year 79 AD, Emperor Zhang of the Han Dynasty summoned many Confucian scholars to meet in the Baihu Temple of Luoyang City. This conference was about the differences between the five Classics. The *Memorandum of the Baihu Conference* (*Baihutongyi*) collected by Ban Gu inherited Dong Zhongshu's theory of the communication between *tian* and human beings. This collection was a short encyclopedia for the New Text School, offering the prophecy and apocrypha cannons. Its thoughts about "Three Ethical Guidelines

Three Ethical Guidelines

A. Emperor is the principal of subjects; B. Father is the principal of son; C. Husband is the principal of wife. This reflects a special ethical relationship between persons in ancient Chinese society. Five constants: 仁 (Ren) kindness; 义 (Yi) loyalty; 礼 (Li) courtesy & rites; 智 (Zhi) wisdom; and 信 (Xin) trust. The five constants are applied to maintain social order and personal relationships.

(*san'gang* 三纲)" and "Six Ethical Principles (*liuji* 六纪)" had a far-reaching impact on traditional Chinese society.

In the *Baihutong*, the idea that the *yang* is superior and *yin* is inferior was developed into human ethical codes. The three ethical guidelines (*san'gang*) are: the sovereign is lord of his subjects, the father is lord of his son, and the husband is lord of his wife. It also brings forth the virtue of a woman called "three followings (*cong*)." This turns Han cosmology into an ethical code and provides a theoretical foundation for the morality of traditional society. It includes relations of agency, human social relationships determining social roles, and ethical codes of practices. The free will of human practice is constrained by one's social relationships.

Huan Tan and Wang Chong's Interpretations of the Cosmos through *Xing* (Nature) and *Qi*

During the transitional era between the Western and Eastern Han (25-220), prophecy and apocrypha were popular. Both emperors, Wang Mang (45 BC-23 AD) and Liu Xiu (6 BC-57 AD), used them to legitimate their reigns and turned them into orthodoxy. Huan Tang (d. 56 AD) was against Liu Xiu's efforts, so he wrote *New Arguments* (*Xinlun*) to criticize the orthodoxy. Huan Tang's famous argument is about the relationship between form and spirit. He compares a candle and fire to body and spirit. From his point of view, fire is reliant on the candle it burns. When the candle burns out, the fire cannot be sustained, so it cannot exist independently. He compares the death of a person to the extinguishing of light to admit that spirits are reliant on materials.

Wang Chong (27-c. 100) was too straight-talking to be a government official for long, so he returned home to write his *Critical Essays* (*Lunheng*). He was an iconoclastic philosopher who distanced himself from the real world. He challenged the arguments of prophecy and apocrypha and deemed himself an opponent of the dominant orthodoxy. He did little to develop

Han cosmology, and typically argued against points rather than supporting them. Nevertheless, he was a great and courageous thinker motivated by his hatred of fictions and falsehoods.

For Wang, the original *qi* is the foundation of the cosmos. *Qi* is a natural material without human will. Everything in heaven and earth is manifested as transformations of original *qi*. *Qi* is self-sufficient, functioning without objectives. Humans and things are generated together with nature in a self-perpetuating manner.

Wang Chong.

Wang considers the myriad things as accidental changes of *qi* in heaven and earth. Heaven and earth do not bring forth human beings with purpose, as a child is born accidentally. A human being is a kind of wise creature that is a continuous part of natural process. Heaven has neither will nor resonance with human affairs. However, Wang replaces the theory of communication between heaven and humans with a view of fate.

The Ontology of Being and Nothingness in the Wei-Jin Dynasties

"Pure Conversations" (*qingtan*) within High-Pressure Political Situations

Beginning with Wei-Jin ontology, Chinese philosophers started to explore the ontological existence of the world through self-awareness, reaching further than the structure of the cosmos in Han Dynasty cosmology. This is demonstrated in studies of the relationship between being (*you*) and nothingness (*wu*) during the Wei-Jin dynasties.

It appears Wei-Jin philosophers did not begin their pursuit of ontological sensibility of "nothingness" simply on account of their theoretical interests. Besides the abundance of political thought inherited from philosophies of the pre-Qin era, the dangerous political struggle caused by shifting from the Han to Wei-Jin dynasties provided a thought-provoking environment for philosophers to explore metaphysical issues regarding ontology, which seemed to have nothing to do with real political practice. Especially during the Three Kingdoms Period (220-280), when the Cao family was in power, Cao Cao (155-220) was a heroic conspirator of the chaotic world, open to adoping various opinions. But, on the other hand, he implemented severe regulations in punishing intellectuals and placed them under repression. Metaphysical debates were brought about through "pure or fine conversations" (*qingtan* 清谈) within high-pressure political situations. Three mystical books: *The Book of Changes*, the *Daodejing*, and the writings of Zhuangzi were very popular in intellectual conversation. The most famous philosophers among those participating were He Yan (c. 193-249) and Wang Bi (226-249).

He Yan was a foster son of Cao Cao and was raised with his other sons, Cao Pi (187-226) and Cao Zhi (192-232). He Yan was clever and talented, so he was envied and not appointed an officer by Cao Pi, who later became emperor. He Yan was not offered any important position until Cao Fang (232-274, r.

The Three Mystical Books

Three philosophical books: *The Book of Changes*, the *Daodejing*, and the *Zhuangzi* were known as "The Three Mystical Books" by the people in the Wei-Jin Dynasties. They were classics of pre-Qin philosophy and became very popular in intellectual conversations among Wei-Jin philosophers.

239-254), Cao Pi's son, succeeded his throne. He Yan was then made secretary of appointments. Together with Cao Shuang, He Yan joined with Sima Yi (179-251) to assist the young emperor. The name for this reign is Zhengshi, and the conversations among intellectuals at this time were called "the Zhengshi metaphysical movement (*zhengshi xuanfeng* 正 夹风)." He Yan was an expert on *The Book of Changes*, *Daodejing* and *Zhuangzi*. He wrote commentaries for *Daodejing* and divided it into the *Classic of Dao* and the *Classic of De*, which influenced Wang Bi's commentaries on the *Daodejing*. As a follower of He Yan from a famous intellectual family, Wang Bi was born to philosophy. From a young age he was very interested in the *Daodejing* and later finished his own commentary. Upon reading this manuscript, He Yan was so astonished he burned all he that had finished. The metaphysical movement was to some extent

The Seven Sages of the Bamboo Grove.

a spiritual liberation movement and a reaction to high political pressure.

The intellectuals of the Wei-Jin dynasties discussed mystics (*xuan*) and *dao*. Most of them were full of inspiration, living libertine lives and composing free-style writings. They aspired to be whoever they wanted to be. Their writings were very personal, countering the Han Dynasty view that human affairs should be consistent with the heavenly *dao*. He Yan was killed in a coup d'etat instigated by Sima Yi. Wang Bi died in the same year. Once Sima Yi came into power, he tried to repress intellectual freedom, and the lives of intellectuals were threatened.

At that time most intellectuals liked to take traditional medicines and drink a lot, such as Ji Kang (224-263), Ran Ji (210-263), Shan Tao (205-283), Xiang Xiu (c. 227-272) and Liu Ling. These men were among the "Seven Sages of the Bamboo Grove (*zhulin qixian* 竹林七贤)" who only enjoyed drinking, secluding themselves in bamboo forests near Luoyang City, playing musical instruments, chanting poems and chatting.

The intellectuals of the Wei-Jin period acted according to pure impulse, but not with any thought of sensuous pleasure. They wished to avoid political entanglement through nonpolitical conversations and debauchery. However, the influence of political power was everywhere, and their plans were thwarted. When Sima Yi, for example, wanted to make Ran Ji an imperial official, Ran Ji got drunk for more than a month. But in the end he still had to serve in office. The death of Ji Kang was an extreme case in which an intellectual was executed over a false charge. There were many other cases in which intellectuals suffered repression, for Chinese leaders lacked political tolerance for those who opposed them.

Wang Bi: Nothingness as the Root of Beings

Wang Bi (226-249) was a genius who died young. He brought forth the metaphysical view that nothingness (*wu*) is the basis for beings (*you*) in his commentaries on the *Daodejing* and *The Book of Changes* (*Zhouyi*).

Wang Bi was influenced by He Yan's book on *dao*, which took *dao* to be nothingness (*wu*). He developed Laozi's idea that "everything was born in something, and something was born in nothing," and brought forth a theory of nothingness being the foundation for everything. From his point of view, *wu* (nothingness) is the source for myriad things, and everything was produced through nothingness. Something must rely on nothingness to be a beginning. The source of myriad things is thus *wu* (nothingness) and not *you* (something). His theory is different from that of Laozi who emphasizes "producing" (*sheng*). Wang holds that the beginning of *you* (something) must be *wu* (nothingness), so *wu* (nothingness) is the root of the existence of things/events.

For Wang Bi, the difference between nothingness and beings is like that between root and end. When a craftsman brings crafts into existence, the craftsman is the root and what he makes is the end. A mother is the root in making children. Wang argues clearly that the myriad things between heaven and earth are based on nothingness. Thus, Wang Bi provides nothingness (*wu*) as an ontological basis for the existence of all things/events.

Wang Bi's *Commentary on the Book of Changes.*

Nothingness (*wu*) is single, and beings (*you*) are multiple. The multiple cannot be the reason for themselves, so they have to rely on "oneness" to lead them. And the root that can lead multiple things is rare. Wang concludes that we should grasp beings as ends by revealing nothingness as their root.

From Wang Bi's perspective, nothingness (*wu*) is not stable, and everything in the world moves without stopping. The changing things cannot serve as an ontological basis, so absolutely immovable nothingness (*wu*) is needed as an ontological basis. Thus, the immovable are found from the movable.

Nothingness is the root and body, so everything else is end and function. The myriad things as functions and representations must have something as their cause. Ontological beings must originate in themselves, and should not rely on anything else. An ontological being is not existent outside anything, but together with the myriad things. This is the philosophical guideline for the continuity of body and function.

Wang Bi argues that nothingness is the root of the world from several aspects: root-end, one-many, moving-immovable and body-function. The sages understand *dao*, take nothingness in their minds and focus on "emptiness." Thus sages ponder the function of nothingness (*wuwei*) though they are situated in powerful positions. In this way, people and things follow their own natures so the whole world will reach an ideal self-perpetuating state through governance without assertive disturbance.

Pei Wei: Taking Being to be Ontological Existence

Pei Wei (267-300) wrote a book titled "On Worshiping Being" in opposition to Wang Bi's idea of taking nothingness as an ontological foundation.

Pei Wei disagrees with Wang Bi's metaphysical view that nothingness is the ontological root for existence, and takes the myriad beings themselves to be the fundamental *dao*. He thinks there are principles in changing phenomena. He takes the change of myriad things and the complicated relationships among them as the principle of things. For Pei, there is principle (*li* 理) in beings (*you*), and one can discover *li* through existence alone.

Pei Wei was against the view that "nothingness can produce beings" and thinks that the first cause was a thing itself. Beings (*you*) are self-fulfilled, so they were not necessarily produced from nothingness (*wu*). Furthermore, since nothingness (*wu*) is absolutely nothing, it cannot be the source for beings that produce everything. He comprehends being and nothingness in an existential sense, believing that being (*you*) is existence, and nothingness (*wu*) is vacant non-existence. In this regard, *wu* (nothingness) cannot be an immutable foundation for existence. According to Pei Wei, *wu* (nothingness) is not an original source, but a state in which nothing exists.

From Pei Wei's perspective, the *li* of the myriad things exists in the relationships among things/events. All things/events are connected with one another, and are interdependent. Thus, everything can serve as a reason for everything else. He raises an idea that "that which supports beings are all beings." For him the mutual support among concrete things/events must be based on "being," whereas "nothingness" cannot account for the existence of things/events.

Wang Bi's theory valuing *wu* (nothingness) is more profound and subtle than Pei Wei's theory of worshiping *you* (beings). But under metaphysical examination, Wang Bi's ontological *wu* (nothingness) is not understood as being exactly nothing in the existential sense Pei indicates. Also, Pei's counter arguments do not seem to breach the existentiality of changing phenomena. They simply take mutual dependence as the foundation for the existence of these phenomena. Pei Wei does not investigate the existential source of the transformation between existence and nothingness. This issue was later solved by Guo Xiang's ontology, viewing being and nothingness as continuous.

Guo Xiang: Being as Obliterating Becoming

Guo Xiang (252-312) concludes the metaphysical debates about being and nothingness. His major work is *Commentary on Zhuangzi*, which was said to be amended on the basis of Xiang Xiu's commentary.

Guo Xiang believes nothingness (*wu*) in the existential sense cannot produce beings, for if *wu* is totally nothing, it cannot produce *you* (beings). Everything is naturally born and self-generating. At the same time, he notices that beings are changing. It is impossible to grasp the myriad beings through changing phenomena, because beings cannot produce beings; they are self-producing. In this way, Guo Xiang holds that everything emerges suddenly and self-creates, generating independently without relying on anything else.

Thus Guo Xiang holds that everything transforms in solitude in a dark remote setting (*duhua yu xuanming zhijing*). He considers this state to have nothing but not to be nothing. The existence of things/events lies in Guo Xiang's dark remote setting, which seems to be vacant but is not total nothingness. In this sense,

Guo Xiang's *Commentary on the Zhuangzi*.

there might not necessarily be any transformation between real existence and absolute nothingness. Since things exist in a context that seems to be nothing, bearing a sense of nothingness and being completely independent, there must be a sensibility of "being qua non-being," suggesting that an object's existence and its dark remote setting mutually produce one another.

The central theme of Guo Xiang's philosophy is that everything transforms in solitude (*duhua* 独化) in a dark remote setting (*xuanming zhijing* 玄冥之境) where things/events exist independently and develop naturally. The myriad things are each secluded in an existential sense; they have no real connection with one another. All things/events transform alone in the sense that they grow and die of their own accord. Transformation in solitude means that everything is alone. People and things are radically independent to the extent that they have no relation with one another. Things/events self-create to be what they are. Everything in the world is temporal and transforms in a rapid changing process.

Existentially, the beings of living reality are left in seclusion, and people are forced to confront a transforming world of nothingness. Guo Xiang portrays the myriad things as changing both naturally and independently, but he does not extrapolate in regard to the feeling one would hold toward the world. The remote and mystical setting does have a sense of beauty beyond words. To develop a life attitude, Guo Xiang integrates Confucian and Daoist views, arguing that a person should act in a Confucian manner while maintaining a Daoist air of mystical thought.

If one wants to understand how to live in a world of lone-transformation (*duhua*), one needs to understand Guo Xiang's thought that experiences lead to destiny. He advises that people keep calm with what they encounter because these encounters themselves lead to destiny. If one must suddenly deal with a variety of new conditions, calmness is the most prudent approach.

From Guo Xiang's perspective, though encountering (*yu* 遇) is contingent, sudden and temporal, it leads to destiny (*ming* 命). Destiny is not any transcendental power from outside, nor is it a pre-determined fate that one cannot change, but a necessary consequence that one has no full control over. Thus, humans and things/events have to follow their destinies. For Guo Xiang, everything is temporal, and one contingent choice might alter the route of life, i.e., the process of destiny. The accumulation of random encounters will gradually change one's life situation, which necessarily evolves into destiny.

Under Guo Xiang's worldview, it is the conflux of random encounters between one and others, or among things/events that changes destiny. Being mystically harmonious (*minghe* 冥合) is one reason for why the myriad things develop independently based on their own natures, running into one another without any reason. Guo Xiang uses "mystically harmonious" to explain that encounters need no reason or arrangements. Destiny is a result of accidental encounters, full of potential that people are unable to control or change. Guo points out that one mystically encounters human destiny, and it is hard to explicate sufficient reasons for it. Guo thus holds that one cannot elucidate this aspect of life because the human life process is a continuous experience full of contingent encountering.

Given that the myriad things are self-creating, things have the autonomy to make choices. However, the self-creating process is full of contingency, since things change in solitude. In a dark remote world, a person is mystically harmonious with things, motivating one to forget oneself as in Zhuangzi's "forgetting oneself in quiet sitting (*zuowang*)." Not only does one need to forget the trace of things, but also the reason why things are as they are. Hence, forgetting oneself means not only forgetting phenomena of the world, but also forgetting the reason for the phenomena. Only in this way can one reach a state continuous with the changes of heaven and earth. Thus, one should calmly accept what one encounters and let random opportunities form a life of necessary destiny.

Guo Xiang developed the debate of being (*you*) and nothingness (*wu*) to its zenith, and thoroughly solved the paradox between necessity and contingency. His philosophy of life naturally developed through his zealous pursuit of metaphysical sensibility of the world. His theory taking beings (*you*) to be nothingness (*wu*) was an important theoretical resource for studies concerning the metaphysics of "emptiness" (*kong*) in Indian Buddhism.

Chinese Metaphysics of Emptiness (*Sunyata*): Buddhism in the Sui and Tang Dynasties

Indian Buddhism was founded by Siddhartha Gautama (called "Sakyamuni" by the Chinese people) in the sixth century BC. He was said to have been destined for a luxurious life as a prince. His father wished for Siddhartha to be a great king, and shielded his son from religious teachings or knowledge of human suffering. As the boy reached the age of sixteen, his father arranged his marriage to a cousin of the same age. Siddhartha spent twenty-nine years as a prince in Kapilavastu. Although his father ensured that Siddhartha was provided with everything he could want or need, Siddhartha felt that material wealth was not the ultimate goal of life. At the age of twenty-nine, Siddhartha left his palace in order to meet his subjects. Despite his father's effort to remove the sick, aged and suffering from public view, Siddhartha was said to have seen an old man. The prince went on further trips where he encountered, variously, a diseased

Buddhist Statues.

man, a decaying corpse and an ascetic. Deeply depressed by these sights, he sought to overcome old age, illness and death by living the life of an ascetic. When Siddhartha was thirty-five he awakened to the Dharma, leaving the sea of suffering under a bodhi tree. In the following forty years, he publicized his enlightened wisdom around the Ganges River, creating the movement of Buddhism.

Siddhartha announced that human life is full of eight sufferings: (1) birth; (2) old age; (3) sickness; (4) death; (5) being apart from loved ones; (6) being together with despised ones; (7) not getting what one wants; (8) the flourishing of the five Skandhas. The causes of these sufferings are karmic effects made by human words and deeds, i.e., the karma of intentions, the karma of speech and the karma of bodily actions. Once one has karma, there are causes, effects and worries. Nirvana is the only emancipation from these worries. There are three paths of this

White Horse Temple in Luoyang, Henan Province.

cultivation: monastic disciplines (*Śīla*), meditation (*Dhyāna*) and wisdom/insight (*Prajñā*).

Indian Buddhism was introduced to China between the Western Han (206 BC-25 AD) and Eastern Han Dynasty (25-220). Emperor Ming of Han (r. 58-75) was said to have dreamed one night in the year 64 of a golden person standing twenty meters tall with a radiating white aureole flying from the West. The next day he told his ministers, and Minister Zhong Hu explained to him that he had probably dreamed of the Buddha from India. The emperor then sent a delegation of eighteen headed by Cai Yin, Qin Jing and Wang Zun to seek out Buddhism. They returned from Afghanistan with an image of Gautama Buddha, the *Sutra of Forty-two Chapters* and two eminent monks. The next year, the emperor ordered the construction of the White Horse Temple three *li* east of the capital Luoyang, to remember the horse that carried back the sutras. It was China's first Buddhist temple. Chinese Buddhist sutras first appeared around 67 AD during the reign of Emperor Ming.

When Buddhism was introduced into China, scholars matched concepts (*geyi* 格义) of Wei-Jin ontology with key terms in Buddhism. For example, in order to comprehend Buddhist *prajñā* (wisdom), Buddhist "being emptiness in nature (*xingkong* 性空)" is matched with nothingness (*wu*), and "revisionary beings (*jiayou* 假有)" with beings (*you*). The central topic for Indian Buddhist metaphysics is "emptiness (*sunyata*)," which was the same for Chinese Buddhist metaphysics. At beginning stages of translating Buddhist *prajñ*, (wisdom) sutras into Chinese, many key terms of Wei-Jin ontology were applied before proper attention had been paid to the original meanings. Not until Kumārajīva's translation of Nagarjuna's Middle Doctrine School did early Chinese Buddhism effectively interpret *sunyata* (emptiness) through *wu* (non-being/nothingness). No longer would a simple relation be drawn between the Indian being/*sunyata* and the Chinese *you*/*wu* (being/non-being).

Seng Zhao: The Founder of Chinese Buddhism

After Kumārajīva arrived in Chang'an in 401, the Chinese Buddhist interpretations of *sunyata* (emptiness) were closer to its original meaning. Seng Zhao (384-414) was praised by his teacher Kumārajīva as the "greatest master of interpreting *sunyata*," and was regarded as the founder of the Chinese Buddhist philosophical system.

Seng Zhao's works were collected in *Essays of Sengzhao* (*Zhaolun* 肇论). His famous arguments are: there is no real unreality; things are immutable; and the *prajñā* (wisdom) knows nothing. He criticizes

Kumārajīva

Kumārajīva (344–413) was a Kuchean Buddhist monk, scholar and translator. He first studied teachings of the Sarvastivada schools, later studied under Buddhasvamin, and finally became a Mahay,na adherent, studying the Madhyamika doctrine of Nagarjuna. He settled in Chang'an. He is mostly remembered for the prolific translation of Buddhist texts written in Sanskrit to Chinese he carried out during his later life.

the earlier theoretical interpretations of Buddhism from the perspective of Wei-Jin ontology. In this way Seng Zhao elaborates the original meaning of the Middle Doctrine School.

From Seng Zhao's perspective, *sunyata* (emptiness/*kong*) is neither real beings nor absolute nothingness. We can neither take non-being (*feiyou* 非有) literally to be no being (*you*), nor can we regard non-nothing (*feiwu* 非无) as really no "*wu*" because both being and nothingness are empty (*sunyata*). He thinks that the idea that taking nothingness as body and things as end in Wei-Jin ontology takes *wu* too literally. However, there is no such ontological non-being (*wu*) above being (*you*). We should feel the *sunyata* (emptiness) of things through the things themselves. Everything is dependent, co-arising with all kinds of conditions, and dependent-disappearing without them. Thus, there is no independent true nature and things are not real beings, so they should be taken as "revisionary beings" (*jiayou*). They are neither real beings nor absolute nothing because they seem to be something. Hence, things/events are not real permanent existence since they are revisionary and actually empty. Thus, being (*you*) and nothingness (*wu*) only differ in name, and both of their ontological statuses are *sunyata* (emptiness).

Seng Zhao argues that the myriad things are not truly existent. They are called "things" under false pretenses. There is a gap between the false indication of these "things" and their real reference. There is no real existence that is correspondent to the names, and names cannot really reflect the function of things. In this way, we cannot understand the *sunyata* of things in existence until we consider them illusory.

Seng Zhao argues that things do not move and counters the common sense view of early Daoism and Buddhism that things are in constant flux. First, he thinks things do not come and go since passing things have disappeared in the past and are not found today. However, the past actually happened, and present circumstances will not revert back to those of the past. In this way we know that past things always stay in the past. Things at present exist today and do not continue to the present from the past. Thus, Seng Zhao maintains that everything stays at present and does not change. Things seem to move but actually do not. Things may transform or eclipse one another, though they do not actually change. As they may transform, people should not stick to anything. One may not hold onto them no matter how strongly they desire to. He provides an example of an old monk, who is the same as the man he was when he was young, but not the same man in regard to his transformation. Therefore, Seng Zhao argues that things at present do not go back to the past and things in the past do not extend to the present. Thus, there is no substantial continuation of things/events through time.

Seng Zhao contends that the *prajñā* [Wisdom of the Buddha, *bore* 般若] is without any knowledge. If one sticks to concrete illusions, one's knowledge is confused intelligence (*huozhi* 惑智), which entails all kinds of worries. For Buddhism, real wisdom is *sunyata,* which is knowledge concerning no particular things or events. This wisdom can thus be called non-knowledge (*wuzhi*).

Eight Monks, Liang Kai, Southern Song Dynasty.

In Seng Zhao's view, if one has certain concrete understanding, one must surely be ignorant about something else. So the highest Buddhist wisdom, *prajñ*, is to realize *sunyata*, an understanding of everything without knowledge of particulars.

Tian-tai School

From the Sui to Tang dynasties, China was reunited and the development of Chinese Buddhism reached its peak. There are many different views about the world in Buddhist metaphysics. The Buddhist schools that had metaphysical contributions and strong influence on later philosophies are: Tian-tai, Consciousness-Only (Weishi) and Hua-yan.

The founder of the Tian-tai (Heavenly Terrace) school was Zhi-yi (538-597) who lived and taught in Tian-tai Mountain, Zhejiang province. His teaching was based on the *Sutra of the Lotus Blossom of the Subtle Dharma* (*Miaofa Lianhua Jing*, commonly abbreviated as *Fahua Jing*). Zhi-yi traced his teachings to Nagarjuna and considered his school to have perfect Buddhist teachings.

Zhi-yi's Threefold Truth includes: the truth of emptiness (*kong-di* 空谛), the truth of provisional existence (*jia-di* 假谛) and the truth of the Middle Way (*zhong-di* 中谛). The truth of emptiness regards all dharma as empty in the sense that they do not have self-nature; the truth of provisional existence regards all dharma as depending on many causal factors to exist. Dharma exist provisionally, temporally, and dependently; the truth of the Middle Way regards all dharma as being both empty and provisional, though meanwhile, they are neither empty nor dependent. Zhi-yi points out that these three truths are harmonious without being contradictory. Thus, he developed Nagarjuna's rejection to attach emptiness or provision to the metaphysics of the threefold truth.

The harmonious threefold truth was integrated with Zhi-yi's view of ten dharma realms. All dharma realms are empty, provisionally existing, and manifesting the Middle Way at the same

Tian-tai Mountain – the headquarters of the Tian-tai sect of Buddhism.

time. They should not be seen as absolute since each one of them penetrates to the other nine realms. For a particular person one intention is one dharma and it penetrates to a hundred realms. Each realm contains three "beings-in-the-world" (*shijian* 兰间), which contain ten "suchness or such-like characteristics (*rushi* 如是)." In this way, one intention contains three thousand suchnesses/worlds (*yinian sanqian* 一念三千). Each intention is integrated with all dharma in harmony and all dharma arise in one intention. Thus is the mystical harmony of intention and the world.

Xuan-zang and the Consciousness-Only School

Xuan-zang (596-664) was the founder of the Consciousness-Only (*Weishi*) School during the Tang Dynasty. Xuan-zang is legendary in Chinese history for having pursued Indian Buddhism at first hand. He became a monk when he was young and soon became devoted to Buddhism. Dissatisfied with conflicting doctrines and errors in translation, Xuan-zang decided to go to India to study the original texts. At first he was not allowed to leave the country. In the autumn of 629 when the capital Chang'an suffered from chaos and famine, he left the country with the starving masses. His aim was to learn Indian Buddhism first hand and to solve the translational problems of Buddhism.

On his four-year journey Xuan-zang encountered many hardships, and some of them nearly cost him his life. Upon arriving in India, he studied at the highest academy of Buddhism for some years and then spent years studying with various Buddhist masters. He brought back 657 Buddhist texts when he returned to China. He devoted some twenty years to complete the translation of 75 texts, more than 1,300 volumes consisting of half-translated Buddhist sutras in the

The relics Nālandā Vihāra of India where Xuanzang once studied.

Xuanzang.

Tang Dynasty. It was said that the translations before Kumārajīva were "ancient translation;" the translations after Kumārajīva were "old translation;" and Xuan-zang's translation was "new translation." Thus, both of these translations of Buddhist scriptures were revolutionary.

The fundamental argument of the Consciousness-Only School is that all Dharma are dependent on consciousness and all things/events are manifestations of intentionality. In a way, intention and consciousness are more important than things/events. There is nothing besides consciousness since everything is in the scope of intentionality.

The world can be divided into two parts: "self," which refers to the subject of life, and "Dharma," which refers to different phenomena. As a subject with intentionality, "self" concerns the whole world, which is *sunyata*. Thus, both "self" and the "dharma" are illusory.

The Consciousness-Only school describes a "threefold nature of existence." This includes the nature of being imagined or conceived to be really existent, the nature of being dependent on others for production, and the nature of perfect, accomplished reality. Most people mistakenly attach to outside things and take the self and dharma to be real existence. What Buddha teaches is that everything is dependent on other things to exist, hence all dharma seem to have manifestations without real nature. The enlightened ones see there is no ontological status underlying the interrelations of dependent co-arising things, so both dharma and self are empty in nature.

Therefore one should give up the attachment

Great Tang Records on the Western Regions

In 646, at the Emperor's request, Xuanzang completed his book *Great Tang Records on the Western Regions* (大唐西域记), which has become one of the primary sources for the study of medieval Central Asia and India. This book was first translated into French by the Sinologist Stanislas Julien in 1857.

to dharma and oneself. One metaphor might be helpful in clarifying this point. A person who sees a rope in the dark might be afraid because he is attached to thinking of the rope as a snake. This is the error of misunderstanding things and wrongly being attached to them. Really the rope is made of fibers that co-arise dependently. To realize perfect, accomplished reality is to eliminate false judgments, such as thinking of the rope as a snake, and to achieve enlightenment.

Fa-zang and Hua-Yan School

Fa-zang (643-712) was the founder of the Hua-Yan School. He enjoyed the strong favor and support of the Empress Wu (r. 684-705) of Tang who gave him the title "Great Master Xianshou." He gave lectures for the Empress Wu on the *Flowery Splendor Scripture* (*Hua-Yan Jing*), and was appointed as a Buddhist leader for the whole nation. He once illustrated key points of Hua-Yan doctrine by using the metaphor of a golden lion. This lecture was composed as *A Hua-Yan Treatise on the Golden Lion*, one of the most important Chinese Buddhist classics. It represents the highest development of Chinese Buddhist metaphysics.

The Hua-Yan School considers its own subtle metaphysics to be "harmonious teaching." It proposes a notion of "dharma realms (*fajie* 法界)," which is a penetration

Fazang, the Great Master Xianshou.

of principle (*li*) referring to the *suntata* of all dharma and events (*shi*). Again, existence is explained through dependent co-arising. There are "four dharma realms": the realm of principle, the realm of events, the realm of the noninterference between principle and events, and the realm of the noninterference of all events. Not only is there noninterference between principles, but also among all events. With water, for example, the waves on its surface are actually none other than water - the waves themselves show the water. The water is not different from waves since the water makes the waves. Waves are just phenomena of water. They are different, yet that does not hinder their continuity.

To illustrate his point that there is noninterference among all events, Fa-zang once used ten mirrors and placed them on eight directions, all facing each other with a lit candle in the middle. This example indicates that there are multiple phenomenal worlds comparable to the unending reflections of mirrors. This demonstrates the unending dependent co-arising of the Hua-Yan school (*huayan wujin yuanqi* 华严无尽缘起).

Fa-zang used his golden lion metaphor to illustrate a similar topic. A golden lion is made from gold and lion, which come into being as the same dependent co-arising causes. The gold and the lion exist simultaneously, all-perfect and complete in their possession. Gold is one and the lion is many. Thus the one and the many are mutually compatible and different. Each phenomenon of the gold lion exists freely and easily, one not hindering or obstructing the other. They are mutually identifiable and thus all dharma exist freely and easily. If we look at the lion as a lion, there is only the lion and no gold. This means that the lion is manifest while the gold is hidden. If we look at the gold, there is only the gold and no lion. This means that the gold is manifest while the lion is hidden. Being hidden, they are secret, and being manifest, they are evident. This is the completion of the secret, the hidden and the manifest.

Chan Buddhism: Enlightening Buddhist Wisdom

The word "Chan" (Zen in Japanese) is a phonetic rendering of the Sanskrit Dhyana, which means meditation. Chan Buddhism of the Tang Dynasty was not satisfied with established systematic interpretations of the world, as held in the Consciousness-Only, Tian-Tai and Hua-Yan schools. On the contrary, Chan discarded their systematic thinking and rebuilt a unique understanding of Buddha nature, enlightening subjects even without the use of words. Thus, Chan Buddhism instigated the shift of Chinese Buddhist metaphysics into epistemology.

The central topic of Buddhism was no longer what the world itself was, but how to understand the world and Buddha's wisdom. In this shift of philosophical paradigm, Chan

Bodhidharma.
Bodhidharma was a Buddhist monk from southern India who lived during the early fifth century. He is traditionally credited as the transmitter of Chan Buddhism to China.

Buddhism succeeded the relationship between mind-heart and things/events with distinct Chinese sensibility, i.e., the continuity of mind-heart and things/events. Chan Buddhism integrated the worldview of Indian Buddhism with epistemology of the pre-Qin era, revealing a unique Chinese philosophical sensibility. This, in turn, provided a starting point for Song-Ming epistemology.

Although its sense of enlightenment is not very profound, the perspective in which it places enlightenment is quite unique. Thus, Chan Buddhism was a turning point in Chinese epistemological history, and it has great significance in linking the Buddhism of the Sui and Tang dynasties with Song-Ming Neo-Confucianism.

Hui-neng (638-713) was regarded as the founder of Chinese Chan Buddhism, which contended that Buddha transmitted his esoteric teaching in private to a disciple. Legend has it that Buddha held a flower in his fingers with a smile. Saying not a word, he confused most of his disciples. But one disciple smiled back. Later Chan Buddhists held that their teaching should be passed from one mind to another, as in accordance with this ancient enlightening episode.

Concomitantly, Chan Buddhism imparts its teachings with methods very different from the words Buddha preached to general assembly. Although the school insisted on teaching without words, many Chan masters composed a variety of documents. However, Hui-neng, the sixth patriarch, was illiterate, and the *Platform Sutra of the Sixth Patriarch (Tanjing)* was the only sutra (classic/*jing*) among Chinese Buddhist classics authored by Chinese monks.

According to the *Platform Sutra*, in order to find out who would be his successor, the fifth patriarch Hong-ren held a contest among his disciples for the verse that best expounded the teaching of Chan. Shen-xiu (c. 605-706), the head disciple wrote his verse as follows:

The body is the tree of enlightenment [the Bodhi tree],
The mind is like a clear mirror-stand.
Polish it diligently time and again,
Not letting it gather dust.

Hui-neng's verse was:

Enlightenment [Bodhi] originally has no tree,
And a clear mirror is not a stand.
Originally there's not a single thing -
Where can dust be attracted?

Comparing these two verses, we can understand that Shen-xiu takes mind, body, and worldly existence as substantial, while Hui-neng takes worldly existence as nothingness, perceiving both body and mind as insubstantial. Hui-neng's insight was found to be much more profound than Shen-xiu's, as his statement "originally there's not a single thing" astonished people later. Hui-neng perceives there is nothing in the world like the light of Buddha's wisdom shining across the darkness of ignorance (*Avidya/wuming* 无明), and opens the path of sudden enlightenment in Chan Buddhism.

According to the *Platform Sutra*, everyone has Buddha nature and their mind-heart is continuous with Dharma. Common people are confused by outside things, which corrupt the harmonious continuity between the mind-heart and things. Most people stick to the difference between bright and shadow, confused by the difference between nature and things, so they cannot clarify their mind and enlighten their Buddha natures. In reality, all Dharma is naturally continuous with original nature.

Hui-neng held that Dharma is inseparable from one's nature, just like the Diamond Sutra's statement: "one's mind should arise naturally without sticking to any attachments." A process operates between mind-heart and nature/natural tendencies. In Chinese, world *xing*/nature is composed of radicals "*xin*/heart-mind" and "*sheng*/generating," so *xing* can be perceived as a moving mind-heart, which is originally clean and quiet. *Xin*/mind or *xing*/nature generates Dharma while seeming unmoved. The reason why the unmoved mind-heart can serve as the origin of moving Dharma is because the co-arising of mind-heart attaches to nothing. Without relation to anything, it is perfectly pure. The heavenly born mind-heart seems to not be moving, but it encompasses everything, so it can cover Dharma. Once the mind-heart has few attachments, it only

The Sixth Patriarch Chopping Bamboo, by Liang Kai, Southern Song Dynasty.

points to "this" or "that" Dharma. At this point it no longer moves as the original mind-heart, and its original Buddha nature is lost.

Therefore, "becoming Buddha when enlightening nature" is actually a realization of the mind's co-arising, letting every intention arise according to heavenly nature. One should not attach to outside illusions or the absolute clean Buddha nature. One should realize the continuity of nature and the mind-heart in the process of a heavenly mind's natural movement. In this sense, *xing*/nature is the body of *xin*/mind-heart, which cannot be separated from the flow of mind. Its nature starts from mind-heart, and they are continuous. They rise in mutual dependence; one's intention leads to the co-arising of nature and mind.

Chan Buddhist epistemology is based on the continuity of mind-heart and Buddha, and so Buddhist wisdom is to perceive unmoving nature through changing phenomena which should not be taken as attachments. Here, the continuity of mind-heart and outer things is a dynamic process, and a sense of unity between mind-heart and Buddha can be sensed in serenity. In perceiving the serenity of moving things, one realizes the continuity of mind-heart and Buddha, and their nature remains pure and clean.

Epistemologically, Chan Buddhism recognizes mind-heart to be continuous with things. There is no essential distinction between mind-heart and things, so it is impossible to discuss how mind-heart connects with things. If there were a distinction between mind-heart and things, the connection could be explained. In this regard, mind would be disturbed by things and not remain in tranquility.

Chan (Zen) Buddhists may practice *koan* (literally "public case") inquiry during sitting meditation, walking meditation, and throughout all the activities of daily life. A *koan* is a story or dialogue, generally related to Chan or other Buddhist history; the most typical form is an anecdote involving early Chinese Chan masters. These anecdotes involving famous Chan teachers are a practical demonstration of their wisdom, and can be used to test a student's progress in Chan practice. *Koans* often appear to be paradoxical or linguistically meaningless dialogues or

Hui-neng, the Sixth Patriarch.

questions. Answering a *koan* requires a student to let go of conceptual thinking and of the logical way we order the world, so that, like creativity in art, the appropriate insight and response arises naturally and spontaneously in the mind. While there is no unique answer to a *koan*, practitioners are expected to demonstrate their understanding of the *koan* and of Zen through their responses. The teacher may approve or disapprove of the answer and guide the student in the right direction. There are also various commentaries on *koans*, written by experienced teachers that can serve as a guide. These commentaries are also of great value to modern scholarship.

For Chan Buddhism, the priority of ontology helps to elucidate continuity of mind and Buddha. One should not keep any ideas that stick to things. Furthermore, one's intentionality should not be attached to literal writings, the cultivation of fortune, or any sort of confusion. The contrast between good and evil should also be abandoned, leaving no attachment to the difference between right and wrong. Thus, the ideal Buddhist realm is "non-intentionality (*wunian* 无念)": no attachment to the degree that one attaches not to a single thing, including emptiness (*kong*). It is one's mind that transforms things, not vice versa. The epistemology of Chan Buddhism concerning the continuity of mind and Buddha serves as an important theoretical resource for the epistemology of Song-Ming Confucianism.

Chinese Epistemology:

Song-Ming Philosophers on the Relationship between Mind-Heart and Things/Events

Compared with the metaphysics of Han and Tang Dynasties, the major contribution of Song-Ming philosophers is epistemology, though they also had great achievements in the area of metaphysics. During the Song (960-1279) and Ming (1368-1644) dynasties, through inquires into understanding heaven and earth, the cosmos or the world, philosophers developed a unique systematic epistemology with Chinese sensibility. Song-Ming epistemology demonstrates that there are many different perspectives for understanding the world in Chinese philosophy.

From Han Yu to Zhang Zai

Han Yu and Li Ao

In the middle of the Tang Dynasty, both Buddhist and Daoist religions were very popular. Being influenced by the transmission of Dharma in Buddhism, Han Yu (768-824) established a theory transmitting the Confucian *dao*.

Han Yu believed the Confucian *dao* was transmitted from Yao [a traditional sage-king of antiquity], to Shun [another sage-king, supposedly the successor of Yao], to Yu [successor of Shun and founder of the Xia Dynasty], to Kings Wen and Wu and the Duke of Zhou [the three founders of the Zhou Dynasty], to Confucius and Mencius. After Mencius, it was no longer transmitted. Han Yu took himself to be the transmitter after Mencius and thought the Confucian *dao* was the *dao* of being humane (*ren*) and appropriate (*yi*): being humane is to love everyone with a spirit of philanthropy; being appropriate is to handle things in a proper way. Han Yu cited the idea of rectifying one's mind and concretizing one's intentionality in the Great Learning to illustrate the difference between Confucian and Buddhist methods of cultivating the mind. His view demonstrated the primary feature of traditional Chinese epistemology.

As a student of Han Yu, Li Ao (died c. 844) created a theory of recovering nature that became the origin of several directions in Song-Ming epistemology:

In learning about nature and destiny (*xingming zhixue* 性命 之学), Li Ao considers the nature of a sage to be quiescent. It is vast, clean and shining between heaven and earth. When it is stimulated, it penetrates all under heaven. From Li Ao's perspective, the *Commentaries of The Book of Changes* and the Confucian classics of the pre-Qin era are real learning about nature and destiny. But Buddhist and Daoist religions are not the proper ways to learn of nature and destiny.

The statue of Han Yu in a temple built in his honor, Chazhou, Guangdong Province.

Li Ao agrees with Zi Si's recommendation for *cheng* (creativity) in *Focusing the Familiar* (*Zhongyong*), and takes *cheng* to be the nature of sages, and the highest realm that a sage can reach. Meanwhile, creativity is also the way to realize the *dao* of nature and destiny. People of his time were normally confused by Buddhist and Daoist religions and did not know that a method of achieving sagehood had already been clarified in ancient Confucian classics.

In recovering nature (*fuxing*), Li Ao agrees with Mencius' argument that human nature is good, and takes the perfect good of human nature to be the foundation for self-cultivation and root for becoming a sage. Sages are not only those who have reached their utmost degree in morality and human relationships, but those who are continuous with the cosmos. Li Ao insists that the purpose of sages' creating rituals and music is to let people forget desires and go back to the proper way of nature and destiny. This is a transformation from the religious meaning of ritual propriety in the pre-Qin era to resurrection of Confucian self-cultivation. Li Ao raises a theory of "recovering nature," taking nature to be good but emotions evil, and nature as the basis for emotions. To recover one's nature is to cultivate oneself by way of abandoning evil emotions as sands are cleaned in water, recovering the original nature of full clarity and purity.

In conclusion, Han Yu and Li Ao brought forth the argument that there were purer and more mature epistemological theories in the pre-Qin era, responding to the challenges of Buddhist epistemology. Their epistemology had a great impact on Song-Ming philosophers. Their thoughts have great significance in the renaissance of contemporary Chinese philosophy. Under the strong influence of Western philosophy, we must learn from Li Ao's examination of ancient Chinese epistemological sensibility, and advance Chinese philosophy to a more mature stage.

Li Ao inquiring the Dao.

Zhou Dunyi

Zhou Dunyi is famous for his article "An Essay on Loving Lotus." His unique philosophical contribution is his epistemological structure of the Great Ultimate (*taiji*) and the Great Ultimate of Human Beings (*renji* 人极). Zhou Dunyi (1017-1073) reconstructs Confucian metaphysics and epistemology, which were embodied in his *Explanation of the Diagram of the Great Ultimate (Taiji Tushuo)*:

In this article, "the Ultimateless (*wuji*) is together with the Great Ultimate (*taiji*)" explains the original state that is beyond description before the distinction of heaven and earth. This original state, being described as something concrete, is the Great Ultimate (*taiji*), but is perceived as being without form or image, the Ultimateless (*Wuji*). The

Zhou Dunyi.

Taiji and *Wuji* are continuous and encompass one another. It is through the being of *Taiji* that the nothingness of *Wuji* is able to be perceived and concretized. When *Taiji* moves, *yang* generates, and its quiescence comes after *yang* reaches its peak. In the *Diagram of the Great Ultimate*, *yangqi* and *yinqi* mutually comprise each other and alternate to be one another. Each one of them relies on its counterpart to exist. The resonance and alternation between *yin* and *yang* generates the myriad things.

Zhou Dunyi's *Taiji-Renji* epistemology serves as the basic structure for Song-Ming epistemology. For Zhou, human beings receive the excellent *qi* from the cosmos, so they are most spiritual. Once the human mind-heart communicates with the transformation of things, *yin* and *yang* are separated and good and evil thus discriminate. In the Confucian tradition, good and evil come after one's intentionality is projected onto what is happening. When sages see complicated human affairs, they devote themselves to the establishment of social sequences for them.

In *Focusing the Familiar (Zhongyong)*, creativity (*cheng*) is not only sincerity, but also the process of humans co-creating with the cosmos, participating in the transformation of things. When humans reach utmost sincerity they can be parallel to heaven and earth, which means that they co-create with the changes of heaven and earth.

In his *Commentaries on Zhouyi (Tongshu)*, Zhou Dunyi takes *cheng* to be the epistemology of *taiji* and *renji* and systematizes it. The beginning of the myriad things is the source of *cheng*. The natures and destinies of things are the unfolding processes of *cheng*. Thus, *cheng* penetrates to the life processes of everything. It has the meaning of originality, but it is not the starting point of any substance. Cheng is a state that is still and quiet, of utmost quiescence. The first movement begins the mystical generation and transformation of the myriad things. Cheng explains these changes as a symptom of propensity (*ji*), which moves

Zhou Dunyi and his *Explanation of the Diagram of the Great Ultimate*.

in a state of no movement, and pacifies in a state of quiescence. Hence, it is with this symptom of propensity that sages restructure human ethics. In conclusion, Zhou Dunyi systematizes his Taiji-Renji epistemology through his elaborations on creativity/cheng.

Shao Yong

Shao Yong (1011-1077) was a famous Zhouyi scholar of the Northern Song Dynasty. When he was young, he studied so diligently that he did not use a stove to keep warm in winters, or a fan to keep cool in summers. He lived as a recluse in Luoyang City when he was old. He invented an enormous system of thought on the image-number school of Zhouyi, and had a great influence on the pre-heavenly Zhouyi studies based on He-tu and Luo-shu from the Song to Qing Dynasty.

Shao Yong's pre-heaven Zhouyi study is rooted in mind-heart, which is both humane and heavenly. He regards mind-heart as the foundation for the originality of the myriad things, and takes everything to be generated from mind-heart. Hence, mind-heart is as important as the Great Ultimate in his philosophy to the extent that heaven and earth and the human mind-heart are continuous and cannot be separated. When the human mind-heart is continuous with the heavenly focus, the dao of heaven and earth penetrates to the dao of human affairs.

The Temple of Shao Yong in Hui County, Henan Province.

In his interpretations of Zhouyi, he takes the pre-heavenly Zhouyi studies to be representations of the human mind-heart, and takes the post-heavenly Zhouyi studies to be the phenomena of all things initiated by the human mind-heart. The *daos* of pre-heavenly and post-heavenly Zhouyi studies consistently penetrate being and nothingness, life and death. This *dao* is as natural and constant as the philosophy of numbers.

Shao Yong holds that one should not use ears or eyes to observe things, but observe them by mind-heart or even patterns (*li* 理). Shao argues that one needs to observe things with a *dao's*-eye-view by enlightening patterns (*li*). This goes beyond any particular perspective, bearing a holistic point of view. Sense organs only observe the form of things. He argues that even water is able to reflect the form of myriad things, but it cannot follow their natures. Sages, however, observe things from the perspective of things themselves, so they can follow the original state of things without being attached to any emotions. Hence their emotional responses to the changes of things are appropriate. Sages can follow the changes of things because they do not have selves. They comprehend the natures of things, realizing that humans are continuous with things in a mystical unity.

Zhang Zai

When Zhang Zai (1020-1077) was young, the Northern Song Dynasty was suffering domestic upheaval and foreign invasion. Zhang Zai submitted a written statement to Premier Fan Zhongyan (989-1052) who was in charge of the border defense set up to fight invaders. Realizing Zhang was a high caliber scholar, Fan persuaded Zhang to return and study *Focusing the Familiar* (*Zhongyong*), which Zhang soon learned a lot from. After studying Buddhism and Daoism, Zhang came back to the *Six Classics* and re-discovered Confucian ideals. Zhang Zai lived a life of philosophical exploration, exerting his utmost effort to establish

Zhang Zai.

his own philosophical system based on his study of *Commentaries of Zhouyi*.

Zhang Zai once lived in the Hengqu County of present Shanxi province, and he was known as Master of Hengqu. He taught in the area of middle Shanxi for a long time, and he was the founder of the Guan School during the Song Dynasty.

Zhang Zai agrees with Mencius' idea that one who fulfills his mind-heart can thoroughly understand his nature/natural tendencies and *tian*. For Zhang, it is impossible to comprehend miscellaneous things/events only based on what one sees and hears. Most minds are confined by what they see and hear, but the sages can enlarge their mind and not be limited by their sense organs, realizing that everything in the world is related to one's existence. Since *tian* is far-reaching without limitations, the confined mind has no ability to embody the wholeness of things, and cannot be continuous with the heavenly mind (*tianxin*).

Thus, Zhang Zai's epistemological theory encourages one to enlarge his or her mind to be continuous with things. He not only admits the rationality of concrete knowing through sense organs, but also emphasizes knowledge through virtues that are not being confined by what one sees or hears. This is an epistemological process starting from enlarging one's inner sincerity, extending to the holistic context of cosmos. Finally, one reaches an inner and outer status continuous with the holistic universe.

Zhang Zai points out that the fundamental task of learning transforms one's original status, i.e., reducing one's post-heavenly status gradually and returning it to the pure good nature of heaven and earth (*tiandi zhixing* 天地之性). Humans have an original status of heaven and earth that is natural, but their post-heavenly habitual *qi* is not pure, so one needs to transform one's character in order to reach what was described in the Western Inscription (*Ximing*). This explains an ideal context in which humans and things are continuous in one great body. The *qi* of one's body is extended fully to the heaven-and-earth, the *qi* of heaven and earth is one's own nature, all people are one's siblings, and the myriad things are one's friends.

One should love all people and beings in the world, living at peace as things come and go. The highest stage of this epistemology is the four-sentence teaching (*sijujiao* 四句教): "Illuminating universal mind-heart for the heavens-and-earth; creating destinies for normal people; succeeding great scholarships from late sages; establishing an ever-lasting peaceful world for generations to come."

The Cheng Brothers and the "Luo School"

Cheng Hao (1032-1085) and his brother Cheng Yi (1033-1107) lived for most of their lives in Luoyang City, so their philosophy was named "Luo School." Cheng Hao was known as Master Mingdao; and Cheng Yi was known as Master Yichuan. These two Cheng brothers initiated the *Studies of Dao* (*daoxue* 道学), which focused on *li* (pattern/principle), and represented the *School of Patterns* (*lixue* 理学) in the Song Dynasty.

Cheng was interested in both Buddhism and Daoism as a young man. Later he studied Confucianism, passed his civil service examinations, and became local officer in many areas. He was dismissed from the government because he opposed the radical reforms of the great innovator Wang Anshi (1021-86). After 1072, he mainly taught his disciples in Luoyang. The two Cheng brothers were different in character. Cheng Hao, the elder brother

Cheng Hao

sat quietly the whole day like a statue, but was very kind when he communicated with people. Cheng Yi, the younger brother, treated others harshly and strictly, so it was harder to communicate with him than his elder brother.

Cheng Hao interprets *tian*/heavens as *li*/pattern, the source of growth and cultivation for all the myriad things. Thus, his *li* is the heavenly *dao*. But the metaphysical *dao* and physical *qi* are only different in name since these two cannot be separated. Cheng agrees with Mencius' idea that the ten thousand things are within oneself, and thinks that if one wishes to realize *dao* one should realize their continuity with things. In this way, one comes to know that the myriad things in the world are related to oneself, and can reach a humane realm full of lively happiness.

Cheng Hao elaborates this humane context in his *On Rectifying One's Mind-Heart* (*Dingxingshu*). For him, the mind of heaven and earth encompasses the myriad things without any real intentionality. The emotion of sages is like this because sages follow the changes of myriad things without letting any emotional responses or intentional feelings affect them. Thus, the mind of a sage is "impersonal and impartial, responding to things spontaneously as they come," without attaching any subjective will or attachments. This is the same line from the *Commentary of Zhouyi*, Mencius, and Chan Buddhism, as well as the epistemologies of Zhou Dunyi, Shao Yong and Zhang Zai.

According to Cheng Hao, both brothers learned from their own self-reflection, though they were taught by some others. The way they presented their philosophy is what distinguished them as philosophers. Their theory on heavenly *li* was philosophically created after their thorough examination and serious study of "embodiment (*titie*)." This, as a feature of Chinese epistemology, is to embody and comprehend with whole heartedness. To embody is to feel, observe, and enlighten through one's own experience, putting one's body into the practice of learning. Finally it comes to know the philosophical *dao*. Embodiment entails a typical methodology of Chinese epistemology, requiring one to be continuous with the *dao* that one learns wholeheartedly.

Cheng Yi

In 1086, one year after Cheng Hao died, Cheng Yi was recommended to be the tutor for the then emperor, who was still a teenager. In order to cultivate the emperor to respect his teacher and culture, Cheng Yi requested that he be allowed to change custom and sit while teaching, and asked for the supervision of the emperor's mother. The emperor was young and liked to play, but Cheng Yi was always serious so he did not communicate well with the emperor. Cheng's harsh behavior made other ministers in court unhappy, and he thus became involved in the power struggle between different parties. After four months, Cheng Yi had to leave the court. Later, he was prosecuted when his school was labeled as a conspirator party. But his students still followed him privately, and he became a pioneer for the movement of *li* (pattern) school.

Cheng Yi argues that the body and its function share the same source, and there is no distinction between the manifested and the obscure. He thinks that the heavenly pattern (*li*) is obscure and not easily clarified, but its images (*xiang*) are miscellaneous and manifested. This view is a typical feature of the continuity of body and function (*ti-yong*) in the Chinese philosophical tradition. In accordance with this, he proposes that neither movement nor quiescence can be regarded as beginning; neither *yin* nor *yang* should be regarded as the origin of the cosmological process. But he also stresses that the initial point of movement is the mind-heart of heavens and earth. For him, moving propensity is the starting point of all movements, so it should be regarded as the root of heaven and earth though there are no concrete limitations for the origin of the universe.

To understand the wholeness of the world is to understand moving propensity as the origin of the cosmological process. Moving propensity is the nascent equilibrium (*zhong*) during which joy, anger, grief and pleasure have yet to arise. The mind-heart, in its ontological sense, is quiescent and does not move. In its functional sense, it penetrates everything if it is stimulated. Cultivating the nascent equilibrium (*zhong*) before emotional responses, and keeping this state of respect is not intentional, but rather it is to prevent intentions from controlling one's mind. This is the foundation for investigating things and acquiring knowledge. However, Cheng Yi emphasizes that patterns (*li*) are in the things themselves, so one needs to investigate them one by one, and reach thorough penetration. This idea was later succeeded by Zhu Xi.

Zhu Xi: Extinguishing Human Desires in order to keep Heavenly Li

Zhu Xi (1130-1200) was the great synthesizer of the school of *li* (pattern/principle). He mostly taught in Fujian province. In his early years, Zhu Xi studied literature, learning a lot from Buddhism and Daoism. He did not start to learn Confucianism until he met Li Tong (1093-1163), who was the third generation disciple of the Cheng Brothers. Li Tong taught him to embody the

heavenly pattern (*li*) in quietude, but
Zhu Xi did not have much experience.
Zhu Xi was later criticized by the
School of Mind for not having enough
embodiment experience. It can be
argued that understanding "Chinese
philosophical sensibility" is not only
a matter of learning classics literally
and interpreting them, but also the
profundity of life experience. Zhu Xi
worked diligently, enjoyed writing
and teaching and accomplished a
tremendous amount of work.

Zhu Xi

Zhu Xi was a successor of the Cheng
Brothers' philosophy of *li*, and took *li* to be the theme
of his own philosophical system. He was invited to
teach the emperor when he was sixty-five. But he was
chased out of court after only forty days due to his
involvement in political struggles. Later, his school was
so harshly wrongly accused that most of his students
did not dare to attend his funeral. Living in sadness
and loneliness, Zhu Xi wrote commentaries for the
Miscellaneous Commentaries Concerning Zhouyi (*Zhouyi
Cantongqi*) in his last years.

From Zhu Xi's perspective, original knowledge is
quiescent without movement, which in the *Zhouyi* is *li*
as a whole body; and in human beings this is a bright
mind-heart. Neither of them is a certain concrete thing.
In Zhongyong this state is a nascent equilibrium in
which joy and anger, grief and pleasure have yet to
arise. In such an extremely empty and quiet state,
the mind penetrates to the changes of image-number
and fortune-misfortune transformation. It seems that

Cheng-Zhu School of Li
(pattern/principle)

Song-Ming Neo-
Confucianism is a form
of Confucianism that was
primarily developed during
the Song Dynasty, but which
can be traced back to Han
Yu and Li Ao in the Tang
Dynasty. It formed the basis
of Confucian orthodoxy
during the Qing Dynasty.
This philosophy attempted
to merge certain basic
elements of Confucian,
Daoist, and Buddhist thought.
The most important of early
Neo-Confucianists was Zhu
Xi (1130-1200).

beings are directly generated from emptiness, while there is no intersection between emptiness and beings. Thus, the continuity of mind and events is just like that of emptiness and beings. This kind of relationship between beings and nothingness is not nothingness and beings as two different stages or states. It is beings directly contained by utter emptiness.

From Zhu Xi's perspective, everything has its own *li* to be what it is. Compared with Lu Jiuyuan and Wang Yangming's idea of *li*, that of Zhu Xi is relatively objective and fixed, which has caused many debates ever since. Song-Ming epistemology basically focuses on how to realize heavenly *li*, which, on the one hand, can be understood as moving, lively, and creative; on the other, it is rather quiet, stable, and unmoving. This debate continued in the twentieth century.

Zhu Xi takes mind-heart to be in charge of one's body, which has spiritual sensibility to respond to things. He quotes the ancient

Wuyi Academy where Zhu Xi once taught.

Zhu Xi's original Meaning of Zhouyi.

Book of History (Shangshu) to illustrate this point. He distinguishes human mind-heart (*renxin* 人心) from the mind-heart of *dao* (*dioxin* 道心). For him, human mind-heart easily goes astray since it makes mistakes when it moves.

Zhu Xi admits the accessibility of *dao*, and thinks there is a particular *dao* that is appropriate for one's nature/natural tendencies. For a particular person there is a proper way to walk in the world, which is original, so one should calmly follow one's own way and work hard in whatever he can accomplish to the highest degree. Then the human road will be extended through the unfolding process of one's intentionality. However, in this extending process, the way that one realizes might be different from the heavenly-mandated *dao*, which is always doubted by humans. This is why the human mind-heart is dangerous. Humans tend to challenge what one has realized about oneself, not walking steadfast along the way but shifting direction according to various situations. But the mind of *dao* is not self-illuminated, and it will not manifest in a natural and necessary way. Thus, the mind of *dao* is subtle and delicate, and the human mind-heart always struggles with that of *dao*.

According to Zhu Xi, the mind of *dao* is transmitted from Confucius. There is a particular *dao* of sages which everyone is expected to follow. If this is true, the *dao* of sages might not be directly related to everyone. But the mind of *dao* should relate to everyone even though it is subtle and delicate and easily confusing. The effort of making the human mind-heart consistent with the mind of *dao* is to maintain a middle way at all times.

In order to pursue the *dao* of sages, one needs to follow sages' teachings, realize the proper way, and be alert to the danger of the human mind-heart. Thus, one needs to fight against one's own dangerous human mind-heart along their way. This is called the effort of "extinguishing human desires in order to keep heavenly *li* (*cun tianli, mie renyu* 存天理，灭人欲)," which is dedicated toward flourishing heavenly *li* in all arising intentions. One should search for the proper way according to oneself,

Yuelu Academy where Zhu Xi once taught.

remain focused and hard working, and fight against one's own desires. Since it is impossible to fully extinguish human desire, people must concentrate on what they should accomplish.

In conclusion, Zhu Xi is the great synthesizer of the *li* school. Zhu takes *li* to be outside the human heart-mind since he stresses that all objective things have *li*. In Song-Ming Confucianism there are two sections concerning the relationship between *li* and things: the *li* school regards *li* to be separable from the heart-mind, while the mind (*xin*) school regards *li* to be continuous with it.

Lu Jiuyuan: The Cosmos does not exist without Mind

Lu Jiuyuan (1139-1193) was from Jiangxi province, and popularly known as the Master of Xiangshan. When he was young he became dissatisfied with Cheng Yi's words and thought "the universe is my mind; my mind is the universe," indicating

that the universe cannot exist independently from the human mind. He also mentioned that whatever happens in the universe is continuous within people's minds. This may be considered a spin-off of Mencius' theory, but Lu mainly created it himself.

Lu Jiuyuan.

Lu Jiuyuan argues that mind is continuous with heavenly pattern/principle (*li*), to the extent that humans share the same *li*.

For him, human minds have remained the same since ancient times. If one can thoroughly understand one's own mind, one is able to be continuous with *tian*. It is in this sense that mind is continuous with *li*. We might argue that *li* is "heavenly nature." Both mind and *li* are not private and concrete, but public and universal. Thus, it is possible that the whole world has one mind in accordance with public *li*. For Lu, the universe can be manifested in one intention, and the *li* of one's mind is penetrable to the whole world.

Like Mencius, Lu Jiuyuan believes the human mind-heart easily deviates from proper way-making because of desires, so one must practice "depriving" in order to manifest one's original mind. The *dao* of learning is to contrast the great mind with the heavenly *li* at first. This is what Lu called "establishing the most important." From Lu's perspective, ancients cultivated

E'hu Academy where Zhu Xi and Lu Jiuyuan once debated.

themselves by keeping their minds and tracing back to their lost mind. This lets original consciousness lead the flux of consciousness and present different aspects of life. If one is able to reach this stage, one's flux of consciousness is like rivers running for the seas that cannot be stopped. Lu himself suggests that one focus on the familiar things at hand, think profoundly in retrospect, and correct one's mistakes in goodness. His teachings were always profoundly influential for his audience.

Lu did not write any books after he took the *Six Classics* to be the outflow of the *li* of mind. Thus, he thought that it was not necessary to interpret the *Six Classics* and advocated a simple effort of introspection. In the E'hu Conference with Zhu Xi in 1175, he contended that his easy and simple effort would last longer than Zhu's painstaking enterprise of ups and downs. He laughed at Zhu's method of learning details first and then reaching sudden enlightenment. Clearly Lu's way of learning was different from that of Zhu Xi since he felt so proud of establishing himself.

Wang Yangming: Nothing is outside one's Mind

Wang Shouren (1472-1528) is generally known as Master Yangming. He is the most prominent philosopher of the Ming Dynasty. He was also a great military general of his time. He once swiftly pacified a rebellion of one of the emperor's vassal kings, and received high honors from the court.

When young Wang Yangming went with his father to Beijing, the capital during the Ming Dynasty, Zhu Xi's works had already been regarded as classics for a long time. As a teenager, Yangming thought a stalk of bamboo must have its own *li* according to Zhu Xi's theory that everything in the world has *li*. Thus, the stalk can be fathomed through the methodology of investigating

Wang Yangming.

things. He asked a friend to sit before a pavilion with him in order to enlighten the *li* of bamboo through investigation. They contemplated before the bamboo for seven days until both of them collapsed. Wang threw doubt on Zhu Xi's doctrine that all things have their own particular *li* after this experience.

Yangming was jailed at thirty-four for presenting a protest paper to the emperor against Liu Jin, the most powerful eunuch in the palace, who was later demoted to the post of house officer. For this Yangming was banished to a remote area called Longchang in Guizhou province, where he was stranded in seclusion. During this low point of his life, he kept studying *The Book of Changes*, learning wisdom of life from it and building a "Den for Pondering over Zhouyi."

One night, he suddenly realized that the *dao* of the sages was all revealed in an idea and astonished his followers. This experience was regarded as "Sudden Enlightenment at Longchang." Through his profoundly shifting life experience, Yangming insisted that the *li* of everything should not be outside one's mind-heart, and Zhu Xi's doctrine was totally wrong.

The pursuit of *dao* in Chinese philosophy is based on experience, so one needs certain experiences to enlighten the profundity of Chinese philosophies. Even great philosophers like Yangming need to suffer a lot before they can understand the depth of theories. After his "Sudden Enlightenment at Longchang," Wang Yangming's zeal was totally refreshed. He taught in many places and recruited many disciples. He could enlighten his disciples like a great Chan master. The Confucian investigation of things was no longer a simple, literal *dao* after his profound transforming experience. After his clarifications, the continuity of mind and things became substantial life wisdom.

The famous story "flowers and trees behind the rocks" (*yanzhong huashu* 岩中花树) illustrates this point. Wang Yangming was once roaming around with some friends. A friend pointed to flowering trees on a cliff and said, "You say there is nothing under heaven external to the mind-heart. These flowering trees on the high mountain blossom and drop their blossoms of themselves. What have they to do with my mind?" The Master answered, "Before you look at these flowers, they and your mind are in a state of indeterminate context [silent vacancy]. When you see them, the flowers as particular actualized foci and your mind as creative context are mutually manifesting and realizing. From this you know that these flowers are not external to your mind."

The flowers and trees remain quiescent in the background behind the stones until someone's purposive intentions resonate with them, manifesting a co-creative context which shapes both the flowers and the viewer. Like the engagement of our minds with the flowers, the unfolding process of mind seems to come into compresence in a one dimensional process, but it is actually a holistic contextual understanding in the arising context of mind. Wang Yangming's story reveals that purpose does not arise from absolute nothingness, but from the immeasurable totality of continuous contextuality. The context of mind is always transforming itself phenomenally, forming a field of existing events. Purposeful actualization is constituted by correlative foci in this field. Yangming's theory of intentionality means to explain the mutually transformative relationship between an unmanifested field of experience and the arising foci of particular events.

Through his battle experience, Yangming imparts his teaching of the continuity between knowing and acting. He points out

Yangming Den in Xiuwen County, Guizhou Province. Yangming once lived here.

with this metaphor: it is easy to kill bandits in the mountains, but it is not easy to correct one's evil intentionality in one's mind-heart. One might not change one's character even if one has endured hundreds of life-and-death battles. One might not conquer oneself even if one is able to lead a big army to conquer lots of enemies. Thus Yangming proposes that what the *Great Learning* taught us is to fathom one's own mind, in the sense that one should correct one's intentions that are not properly consistent with heavenly patterns, and try one's best to lead one's mind onto the correct path. One should work hard to conquer the short-comings in one's mind even though it is difficult to correct evil intentions and desires.

It is important to correct evil intentions before they arise in one's mind-heart. Like a good deed, it is proper to put one's intentionality on the proper track. When one's intentions are correct, they extend toward others in an appropriate manner filled with heavenly principles. Human affairs in the world begin with intentionality, so if one is afraid that one's intentions might lead to bad responses, one should be cautious about one's intentionality at the very beginning. For Wang, humans naturally follow their inner judgments about good and bad and act accordingly, so it is impossible to separate knowing from acting. In order to cultivate oneself, a person should carry out one's cultivating efforts of promoting good and avoiding evil

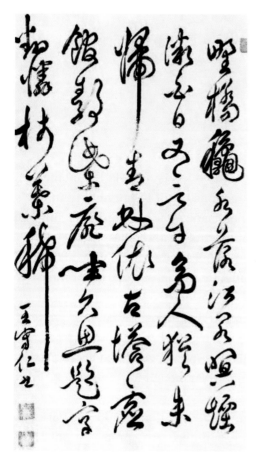

Wang Yangming's handwriting.

intentions just like a person naturally likes beauty and dislikes ugliness.

In traditional Confucian thought, to realize the *dao* of sages is the main task of philosophers. Philosophers continued to study the *dao* of sages, carrying on the daunting project of transmitting "this Chinese culture of ours (*siwen*)." They continued to illuminate the *dao* of sages as much as was possible. After the mid-Ming Dynasty, several philosophers devoted their lives to the mission of preserving the traditional *dao* of sages.

The *Dao* of Chinese Philosophy:

Its Sustainment and Creativity

The question of whether Chinese philosophy is "philosophy" has long haunted researchers in modern China. I would argue that there was "philosophy" in ancient China, though it was not as exactly the same as "philosophy" in the West. Ancient Chinese philosophers had a profound philosophical sensibility and conducted theoretical debates about it. This can be compared to the history of Western philosophy. The classification of Chinese thought is disputed because ancient thinkers lacked understanding of Western philosophy, and they were not cognizant of their own philosophical sensibility. For this reason, researchers today do not recognize ancient Chinese philosophical sensibility as "philosophy."

A group of Chinese intellectuals devoted themselves wholeheartedly to the *dao* of Chinese philosophy, and their devotion to theoretical construction can be seen in parallel to that of Western philosophers. Since the introduction of Western philosophy during the Ming and Qing dynasties, the confidence in traditional Chinese theoretical construction has been greatly shaken. But there were still many philosophers who devoted their lives to the *dao* of traditional Chinese philosophy.

Three Philosophers between the Ming and Qing Dynasties

Let's begin with the thinking of three prominent philosophers who sustained the *dao* of Chinese philosophy between the Ming and Qing dynasties. We can examine how Chinese philosophers responded to Western philosophy on the grounds of traditional *dao*, and how they created a new enterprise for the Chinese philosophical *dao* in Chinese-Western comparative philosophy.

Huang Zongxi

Huang Zongxi's (1610-1695) father was a member of the famous Donglin Party in the late Ming Dynasty, and was prosecuted and executed because of his protest against the powerful eunuchs at the court. Zhu Youjian (1611-1644), the succeeding emperor, removed those eunuchs who had killed Huang's father and others. At the age of nineteen, Huang Zongxi was filled with both hatred and courage. He travelled to the capital to avenge his father and stabbed a eunuch who had been responsible for his father's death.

The Ming Dynasty collapsed in 1644 when Li Zicheng occupied Beijing and the last emperor committed suicide. Huang organized an army and fought against the Qing Dynasty for about eight years. Not until 1653 did Huang come back to his study to write his masterpieces. Among them are two scholarly histories of the Song, Yuan and Ming dynasties.

Huang holds that the mind-heart and cosmological *qi* are continuous, and that they only differ in name. He argues that mind fulfills the whole universe and the world is the representations and transformations of the mind. Meanwhile, he takes the mind as cosmological *qi*, arguing that humans were born of *qi* and the mind is the subtle and mystical function of

Huang Zongxi.

qi. Thus, wherever *qi* moves, mind manifests itself. In this sense, the movement of *qi* is the flow of mind, and the mystical functions of *qi* are manifestations of mind. He agrees with Wang Yangming that mind penetrates to the myriad things and insists on the continuity between patterns of things and mind. Thus, one should investigate the pattern of mind if one wants to clarify the pattern of things. For him, the pattern of mind is mystically changing and manifesting in various forms. There is no substance for mind, and the highest status one can reach is the original state of mind. This is a methodology of establishing ontological status (*ti*) through functioning (*yong*). From Huang's perspective, there is not only knowledge of objective existence, but also knowledge inherited from heaven, including a comprehensive understanding of the world.

Huang suffered much when he was young and developed harsh criticisms of the autarchic regime. He once wrote a book that is sometimes considered a declaration for human rights in seventeenth-century China. He argued that all people were self-absorbed in ancient times, and their leaders were those who helped the community develop public interest and eliminate public enemies. However, later leaders wanted to monopolize all advantages and inflict disadvantages onto others. They took themselves to be masters of the community, and all people as their guests. Accordingly, they called themselves "servants of the community," while they took all under heaven to serve their own interests and worked against the community. Huang also believes that ministers should not only work for their masters, but bear in mind the happiness and worries of their own people. He advocated freedom of speech, considering schools to be a place for debating public issues like a modern parliament.

Huang's greatest idea was "people are masters and ministers their guests." However, it was very difficult to achieve this at any time. In an environment focused on selfish interests, dreams of idealists were doomed to fail. However, idealists were able to lead people to make progress because their dreams remained as timeless ideals.

Huang edited two historical documents of Neo-Confucianism from the Song to Ming Dynasty, which are the most important sources for scholarship today. These two scholarly histories not only serve as the basis for Song-Ming intellectual history, but also as testimony to the sustainment of Chinese philosophical *dao*.

Fang Yizhi

Fang Yizhi (1611-1671) was one year younger than Huang Zongxi. He once worked in the emperor's academy during the late Ming Dynasty. Fang fled to South China after the Ming Dynasty collapsed, then to the Guangdong area because of prosecution from ministers. He cut his hair and became a monk in 1650 when the Qing army entered the cities of Guiling and Guangzhou. As a recluse, he completed some philosophy works in his later years.

Fang Yizhi was openly receptive to Western scholarship, introduced into China in the later years of the Ming Dynasty. Fang Yizhi communicated often with missionaries such as Johann Adam Schall von Bell (1591-1666). He wrote a small scientific book based on his understanding of Western science, where he quoted various studies of Western natural science. He was the

Johann Adam Schall von Bell

Johann Adam Schall von Bell (1591-1666) was a German Jesuit missionary to China. Born to noble parents in Cologne, Germany, he attended the Jesuit Gymnasium and joined the Society of Jesus in Rome in 1611. In 1618 he left for China, reaching Macao in 1619. Apart from successful missionary work, he became the trusted counselor of the Shunzhi Emperor of the Qing dynasty, was created a mandarin, and held an important post in connection with the mathematical school. His position enabled him to procure from the emperor permission for the Jesuits to build churches and to preach throughout the country. The Shunzhi Emperor, however, died in 1661, and Schall's circumstances at once changed. Astrologer Yang Guangxian alleged he indirectly caused the death of Empress Xiao Xian. Schall was imprisoned and condemned to death. The sentence was not carried out, but he died after his release owing to the privations he had endured. A collection of his manuscripts was deposited in the Vatican Library.

Johann Adam Schall von Bell, a
German Jesuit missionary to China.

first Chinese citizen to distinguish the heart-mind from the brain, taking human spirits to be a function of the brain instead of the heart. From this he determined that intelligence is determined by clarity of the brain.

Fang Yizhi had a profound understanding of traditional Chinese epistemology, believing the mind-heart and things/events are continuous. He holds "there is nothing without one's mind, and there is no mind without things." He admits the existence of things between heaven and earth, and he stresses that one's mind is penetrable to all things under heaven, making minds and things continuous. Hence, he takes time and space to be continuous in the sense that they are contextualized with one another and cannot be separated.

By the same token, Fang Yizhi takes mind-heart to be a meaningful concept that is penetrable to *taiji*, *tian*, *xing* (nature) and *ming* (destiny). This touches the dilemma of Chinese epistemology, which applies various concepts to represent similar philosophical meanings. Philosophical sensibility is most demonstrated in his view that mind and things are continuous, especially in his theory that the "public mind" (*gongxin* 公心) is the foundation for views such as "everything arises through mind-heart." As for the relationship between the *qi*, *li* and *xin*, Fang thinks the mind is the basis of cosmological *qi* and *li* (patterns), which are continuous with one mind.

Wang Fuzhi

Wang Fuzhi (1619-1692) was concerned about his era and strived to change society when he was young. When he was twenty-five years old, his father was kidnapped by Zhang

Xianzhong's army. In order to save his father, he pretended to be seriously ill by harming his own body. He swopped places with his father, and then managed to flee to safety. In 1648, he organized an army to fight against the Qing Dynasty in Hengyang City. In defeat he was prosecuted by vice ministers in the court of the Late Ming Dynasty. Wang opted for seclusion in present Hunan province even after the peasants' rebel army victory in 1652. He was known as Master Chuanshan. He wrote commentaries on *Zhouyi, Daodejing*, and other major philosophical classics. With the spirit of Sisyphus, Wang Fuzhi devoted himself to the *dao* of Chinese philosophy in loneliness.

Wang Fuzhi

In responding to the epistemology of Wang Yangming, Wang Fuzhi considered actions *a priori* to knowledge, meaning it is easy to know but difficult to act. For him, it is possible to carry out actions with knowledge. Knowing and acting are functions for one another. He criticized Yangming's idea of the continuity of acting and knowing, saying it took knowing to be acting. Its influence reached even his followers in the Late Ming Dynasty, who enjoyed talking and practicing without any solid grounds.

Wang Fuzhi succeeds the *qi* cosmology of Zhang Zai and takes *qi* to be the Great Emptiness (*taixu* 太虚) that is continuous with *qi*. Nothingness is compared with beings; there is no absolute nothingness. *Li* (pattern) resides in *qi*, and the movement and pattern of *qi* changes all the time. Thus, all under heaven are concrete particulars (vessels /*qi* 器), and *dao* is not beyond any tangible existence. The pattern/principle (*dao*) is always together with physical bodies. In the same way, it is impossible to view pattern/principle (*dao*) as something beyond material substance. So there is no pattern/principle (*dao*) outside or behind phenomenal images.

Wang Fuzhi uses creativity (*cheng*) to argue his cosmological view of the continuity of Great Emptiness and substantial existence. Thus, the substantial particulars in Great Emptiness always

A Treatise on Reading Tongjian by Wang Fuzhi.

move no matter if it is viewed to be moving or not. Their movement and non-movement are continuous. Hence, this original-happening momentum pushes things to move forward. He asserts that human habit develops with growing natural tendencies, so human nature is not only heavenly inherence, but also a dynamic process that is changing daily and completing.

Wang Fuzhi was a great synthesizer of ancient Chinese philosophy. His philosophical system was a concentration of the ancient Chinese philosophical *dao*. His philosophy was a detailed unfolding process of epistemology and metaphysics before the Han Dynasty. Before the introduction of Western philosophy, his philosophical system represented the highest achievement of traditional Chinese philosophical sensibility.

Modern Chinese Philosophy as responses to Western Philosophies

Modern Chinese philosophy can be seen as a response to the strong influence of Western philosophy. After the Opium War in the mid-nineteenth century, China was very weak and cultural conflict between China and the West first emerged. Modern Chinese philosophers, such as Zeng Guofan, Kang Youwei, Liang Qichao, Zhang Taiyan, Yan Fu and Wang Guowei were concerned with the chaotic situation and searched for solutions to sustain "this Chinese culture of ours."

In the late Qing Dynasty, the renaissance of pre-Qin philosophies challenged the orthodoxy of Confucianism. Zeng Guofan (1811-1872) advocated that Confucianism should communicate with pre-Qin philosophies in order to survive the impact of Western culture. He acknowledged the value of Song-Ming Neo-Confucianism, which was taken as a foundation for him to reinterpret the meaning of traditional Confucianism. He tried to search for a common ground for Han and Song scholarship and incorporate merits of different scholarships, but did not have much insight into them. Later, officials like Zhang Zhidong (1837-1909) promoted an idea of "Chinese body and Western function" in order to fulfill the idea brought forth by Wei Yuan that the Chinese

Zeng Guofan.

Kang Youwei.

must learn from Western powers in order surpass them.

As the organizer of a reformation movement which was supported by the Guangxu Emperor in 1898, Kang Youwei (1858-1927) wanted to establish constitutional monarchy in old China. After the movement failed, he fled abroad for some years. Later, he became a loyalist of the feudal system, promoting the idea of Confucian religion. Because he wanted to make Confucianism a state religion, he was attacked by revolutionists and supporters of the New Cultural Movement.

Kang Youwei developed the pragmatism in contemporary studies on ancient classics to its extreme. His works, such as *Textual Research of the False Classics of Xinxue* and the *Research on Confucius' Reform,* had a strong influence on intellectuals in the late Qing Dynasty. He depicted Confucius as a revolutionist and a supporter of constitutionalism. He wanted to establish constitutional monarchy through promoting his new interpretation of Confucianism. This was certainly a radical reconstruction of Confucianism. His idea aroused astonishment and fear among old-fashioned intellectuals, who asked the government to burn Kang's works.

After the failure of the reformation movement in 1898, Liang Qichao (1873-1929) fled with Kang Youwei to Japan. However, Liang, the former student, diverged in opinion from his tutor

Liang Qichao.

Zhang Taiyan's letter to Lu Xun.

as the situation changed. Liang considered freedom of thought to be the most important thing for China at that time. Therefore, he devoted himself to enlightening common people to cultivate a sense of public and state. However, Liang was a sensitive thinker and his thought underwent many changes. For example, during his trip to Europe, he noticed many societal problems in the aftermath of World War I. Upon his return, he became a modern conservative and advocated traditional Chinese thought.

If Kang Youwei can be regarded as the representative of modern studies on classic learning, then Zhang Taiyan (1869-1936) might be considered as the representative of traditional studies on the classic learning. Zhang was very actively involved in social movements and wanted to change society. In 1903, he was thrown into prison for writing an article titled "On Advocating Revolutionary by Criticizing Kang Youwei" and a preface for Zhou Rong's book titled *Revolutionary Army*, which promoted revolutionary thought and irritated the imperial government of the Qing Dynasty. He became a member of the Tongmeng

Organization led by Sun Yat-sen after he was released in 1906. He was an advisor for Sun's new republic government in 1911. He participated in the anti-Yuan Shikai movement and was under house arrest till Yuan's death.

Zhang's major contribution was on the studies of ancient classics and thoughts. He incorporated Western thoughts and developed a "Theory of Two-way Evolution," which means the good and evil sides of things evolve together. He advocated pure traditional Chinese culture but he did not worship Confucius. He was one of the key figures in the transformation of modern scholarship.

The Jesuits first introduced philosophy as a discipline in China in the late Ming Dynasty. Many Chinese students went to Japan to study in the late Qing Dynasty and brought back lots of Western philosophical ideas which are still popular today.

The most influential figure who introduced Western philosophy to the modern era of Chinese history was Yan Fu (1854-1921). Yan went to England to study naval technology

Yan Fu's old residence in Fuzhou, Fujian Province.

when he was young, and later his interest shifted to Western political institutions and culture. He translated T. H. Huxley's *Evolution and Ethics* with great enthusiasm in 1895, and continued to advocate evolutionary theory. Yan considered Western political and economic institutions and modern scientific progress as the reasons for their wealth and power. He appreciated British Empiricism and criticized Wang Yangming's idea of innate knowledge, wishing China would welcome the scientific attitude of studying and understanding things. He always added his own

Wang Guowei

comments in his translations. He agreed with Xunzi and Liu Yuxi of the Tang Dynasty that the heavens and human beings are separable, so human beings should have their free will. He tried to call on the patriotism of Chinese people and to promote revolutionary movement when China was experiencing radical transformations.

Wang Guowei (1877-1927) first introduced the system of Western philosophical thought, and applied its framework to explain Chinese philosophy. He committed suicide by jumping into the Kunming Lake in the Summer Palace, and this became a notable event among intellectuals of that day.

Wang was fascinated by Arthur Schopenhauer's thought when he was young and spent many years learning and translating Western philosophy and developing a good sense about it. He enjoyed reading Schopenhauer and Kant's philosophies, and rearranged Chinese philosophical data with Western philosophical framework. For example, he applied terms like "metaphysics" and "ethics" when writing about Confucius' thoughts.

Wang argues that it might be difficult to claim that there is a whole body of knowledge that corresponds to Western philosophy in ancient Chinese scholarship, but there was indeed some knowledge which could be called "Chinese philosophy." He criticizes Gu Hongming's translation of *Zhongyong*, and claims that it is nearly impossible to translate the core Chinese philosophical concepts into other languages. The questions he raised remain unavoidable in the realm of Chinese and Western comparative philosophy today.

Modern Chinese Philosophy:

New Confucianism and East-West Comparative Philosophy

As both an idea and a discipline, modern Chinese philosophy was established under the challenge and impact of Western philosophy. In the process of constructing Chinese philosophy, Hu Shi (1891-1962) and Fung Yu-lan (1895-1990) were pioneers in establishing Chinese philosophical systems. Both of them received PhDs from American universities. Being influenced by Westerners' denial of Chinese philosophy, they devoted themselves to constructing models of Chinese philosophical history. Before them, Wang Guowei was strongly influenced by Schopenhauer's philosophy. From Wang's perspective, China did have its own philosophy, though it was difficult to find exactly the same counterpart of Western philosophy in the Chinese intellectual tradition.

道 不 远 人

——比较哲学视域中的《老子》

〔美〕安乐哲（Roger T. Ames）郝大维（David L. Hall）/ 著
何金俐 / 译

Hu Shi, Fung Yu-lan, and the discipline of Modern Chinese Philosophy

Hu Shi went to Columbia University to study philosophy in America. At Columbia he was greatly influenced by his professor, John Dewey. He became a professor at Peking University and one of the leaders in the New Cultural Movement. Hu helped Dewey in his 1919-1921 lectures series in China, and was a lifelong advocate of pragmatic evolutionary change. Hu was a staunch supporter of pragmatism and advocated cultural reform only under the guidance of pragmatism.

Hu Shi.

Hu Shi wrote *An Outline of Chinese Philosophy*, of which he only finished the first half. However, this was the first history of Chinese philosophy with historical materials complied and interpreted according to the methodology of Western philosophy. It threw off traditional scholarly structure, and was influential on contemporary research of Chinese philosophy.

When Fung Yu-lan studied at Columbia University, he realized that Westerners knew little about Chinese philosophy. Upon his return to China, he accomplished *A History of Chinese Philosophy*, establishing a comprehensive system of Chinese philosophy. He arranged and analyzed Chinese philosophical materials according to branches of Western philosophy, discovering parallels between ancient Chinese literature and Western philosophical topics. For scholarly relations between China and the West, Fung's *History of Chinese Philosophy* serves as a useful resource for the discovery of Chinese philosophical materials.

Hu Shi's *An Outline of Chinese Philosophy*.

Fung Yu-lan and his daughter Zong Pu.

For metaphysics, Fung Yu-lan constructed the New School of Li (*xin lixue* 新理学), his own philosophical system. He regards pre-Qin Daoism, Wei-Jin ontology, Chan Buddhism and Neo-Confucianism as substantial foundations for Chinese metaphysics, which embody the spirit of Chinese philosophy. He presents his "New School of Li" as a continuation of Song-Ming Neo-Confucianism. The reason why his philosophy should be called "New School of Li" is because he explores metaphysics in a new direction. Fung argues that his *li* is similar to Zhu Xi's *li* and Plato's ideas. It can be argued that Fung's philosophical sensibility is derived from Wei-Jin ontology, and his systematic structure takes after Cheng Yi-Zhu Xi's school of Neo-Confucianism.

In his later years, Fung Yu-lan wrote a new edition of his *History of Chinese Philosophy*, and rearranged the historical documents of Chinese philosophy. Fung's contribution is both historical and philosophical because he relied on Chinese philosophical materials and established his own philosophy based on his training in Western philosophy. His system of Chinese philosophy was a milestone for the advancement and proliferation of Chinese philosophy throughout the world.

Xiong Shili and New Confucianism

Xiong Shili (1885-1968) was the most original Chinese philosopher of twentieth-century China. He was born into the poor family of a countryside teacher, and had to watch herds to make a living at only eight years of age. He devoted himself to the revolutionary movement for about ten years after his father died young. He decided to part from the movement after witnessing bloodshed among party members, forcing him into depression. He soon devoted himself completely to learning. Upon visiting Zhou Dunyi's memorial place, Xiong made up his mind to become the second Zhou of his time. Xiong had a strong will to establish a new generation of learning like Zhou, who initiated the metaphysics and epistemology of Song-Ming Neo-Confucianism. Parallel to Zhou's achievements, Xiong was the founder of metaphysics and epistemology for modern Confucianism.

Beginning in 1920, Xiong studied Buddhism for three years with Ouyang Jingwu (1871-1943), a great master of Buddhism in Nanjing. Xiong lived poorly but worked extremely hard. He was recognized by Cai Yuanpei (1868-1940) and invited to Peking University to lecture on the Consciousness-Only School of Buddhism in 1922. He published *A New Treatise on the Consciousness-Only School* in 1932. This book was criticized by his previous Buddhist teachers and fellow students, but it was also praised by many famous scholars of his time, such as Cai Yuanpei, and Ma Yifu (1883-1967).

The fundamental topics of Xiong's *A New Treatise on the Consciousness-Only School* are the continuity of mind-heart and things/events, the unity of body and function, and the inseparability of ontological status and phenomena. From Xiong's perspective, the fundamental problems of Western metaphysics are the separation of ontological status from phenomena, separating mind-heart from things/events, subject from object, human life from the cosmos, ideal from actuality and so on. This separation leads to the theoretical dilemma of transcending phenomena to explore substance. Chinese metaphysics manifests ontological body through function, making the body and function continuous, and ontological status is unceasingly changing with phenomena.

For Xiong, universal mind and the minds of concrete particulars are continuous, thus this kind of ontological mind can be called "original mind" (*benxin* 本心) or "humane mind" (*renxin* 人心). Ontological status functions through both the opening and closing of intentionality. For concrete particulars, Xiong emphasizes the creative function of mind, taking the cosmos to be a concretizing process of one's intentionality. He starts with traditional views of the continuity of heaven and human beings, and

Ouyang Jingwu

Ouyang Jingwu was born in 1871. His original name was Jian, and his alias was Jinghu. When he was forty, he used a new alias, Jingwu, which became better known as he became famous in Buddhism. In July 1922, he established the China Self-Education College in order to conduct research, teach, and propagate Buddhist culture. Theoretically, he promoted the Consciousness-Only School of Buddhism. He devoted all his life to Buddhist research, rearranging Buddhist sutras and Buddhist education, and became one of the most famous Buddhist thinkers in modern Chinese history.

the inseparability of *dao* and cosmological *qi*, and argues for the continuity of ontological body and function, as well as the continuity of mind and things. In this way he developed traditional philosophical sensibility to its fullest. Without any training in Western philosophy, Xiong agrees with the metaphysics of Whitehead and Bergson, and elaborates on Chinese philosophical sensibility with accuracy and acuity.

After Xiong Shili, a communicating crosscurrent was formed when Chinese philosophy, with Confucianism as its main body, continued its dialogue with Western philosophy.

Liang Shumin (1893-1988) wanted to integrate Confucianism with Wang Yangming's thought, utilizing Buddhism and Bergson's philosophy of life. He took "will" to be the root of cosmos, and combined the Chinese philosophical tradition of

The inscription on Laing Shumin's tomb.

unceasing generation with modern evolutionary theory. Liang was a new Confucian philosopher who attempted to demonstrate the relevance of Confucianism to China's problems in the twentieth century. A believer in the unity of thought and action, Liang became a leader in attempts at peasant organization. Originally a Buddhist, Liang in 1917 was appointed to the faculty of Peking University as the first professor of Buddhism ever to serve on the staff of a Chinese university. He attempted to demonstrate to an increasingly iconoclastic and Westernized Chinese intelligentsia the modern relevance of Chinese, especially Confucian, culture. Characterizing the Western attitude as one of struggle, the Chinese attitude as one of harmonization through adjustment, and the Indian attitude as escapist, Liang theorized that after World War I, Western culture was dominant; this phase, he claimed, would soon be replaced.

Mu Zongsan (1909-1995) was a Chinese New Confucian philosopher. His thought was heavily influenced by Immanuel Kant, whose three *Critiques* were translated by him into Chinese. He then retranslated Kant's works, trying to incorporate Confucian philosophy into Kantian philosophy, and in doing so constructed a Confucian "moral metaphysics." Over the last forty years of his life, Mou wrote histories of "Neo-Daoist," Confucian, and Buddhist philosophy as a group of constructive philosophic treatises, culminating in his work *On the Summum Bonum* (*yuan shan lun* 圆善论) in 1985. He attempts to rectify the problems in Kant's system through a Confucian-based philosophy reworked with a set of concepts appropriated from Tian-Tai Buddhism. Mou is especially famous for his cultural traditionalism and his defense of democracy as a traditional Chinese value.

Tang Junyi (1909-1978) was one of the leading exponents of New Confucianism. He was influenced by Plato and Hegel as well as by earlier Confucian thought. Born in mainland China,

Tang Junyi went into exile in Hong Kong in 1949 and lived there for the rest of his life. There he helped found the New Asia College, which was integrated into the Chinese University of Hong Kong in 1963. Tang established a humane realm of moral idealism based on his understandings of Chinese and Western philosophies.

Thome H. Fang (1899-1977) merged the philosophies of life in both China and the West based on Confucianism, promoting the Confucian attitude of unceasing generation. From 1925 to 1948, Fang taught at several universities in China, mostly at the National Central University in Nanking and Chungking. Then he taught at National Taiwan University.

Contemporary East-West Comparative Philosophy

In the English-speaking world, Wing-tsit Chan (1901-1994) was one of the founders of the philosophy department at the University of Hawaii, the first department in the West to bring Chinese philosophy into the limelight. Chan translated much Chinese philosophical literature into English and was one of the world's leading scholars of Chinese philosophy and religion. Chan was born to a peasant family in rural area of southern China. After graduating with a bachelor's degree from Lingnan, he began his graduate studies at Harvard University in 1924. He received his Ph.D. in Philosophy and Chinese Culture in 1929. On his return to China in 1929, Chan received an appointment at Lingnan, which in 1927 had been reconstituted as Lingnan University, and served as its Dean of the Faculty from 1929 to 1936. In 1935 the University of Hawai'i offered him a visiting appointment. In 1937 he moved to Honolulu and taught there until 1942. He then taught at Dartmouth College from 1942 to 1966. Chan was the author of *A Source Book in Chinese Philosophy*,

The First World Confucian Conference was held in Qufu, Shangdong Province on September 27, 2008. Conference participants were from China, Korea, Singapore, the USA, UK, France and Australia.

one of the most influential sources in the field of Asian studies, and of hundreds of books and articles in both English and Chinese on Chinese philosophy and religion. He was a leading translator of Chinese philosophical texts into English in the twentieth century. The W.T. Chan Fellowship Program was established in his memory in 2000 and fellowships are awarded annually to students who are devoted to Chinese and comparative philosophy.

Wei-ming Tu (1940-) is the main leader in the revival movement of modern Confucianism. He hopes to adjust the Confucian tradition for modern times. Tu is an ethicist and a New Confucian scholar. Tu was Harvard-Yenching Professor of Chinese History and Philosophy and of Confucian Studies in the Department of East Asian Languages and Civilizations at Harvard University. He was Director of the Harvard-Yenching Institute (1996-2008) and Director of the Institute of Culture and Communication at the East-West Center in Hawaii (1990-1991). He is a fellow of the American Academy of Arts and Sciences. Tu was born in

Kunming, Yunnan Province in 1940. He has been on the Harvard faculty since 1981. Tu is concerned with the modern fate of Confucianism, and devotes his life to promoting the modern meaning of Confucianism in order to help traditional Chinese culture dialogue with modernity in a new historical era.

Chung-ying Cheng (1935-) is a philosopher and professor of philosophy at the University of Hawai'i at Manoa. He received his BA in 1956 from National Taiwan University, his MA in 1958 from University of Washington, and PhD in 1964 from Harvard University. He serves as Editor-in-Chief of the *Journal of Chinese Philosophy* published by Blackwell Publishers. Cheng is the founder of "onto-hermeneutics," analyzing the ontological status of Chinese philosophy in a Chinese-Western communication milieu.

Daodejing: Making This Life Significant, by Roger T. Ames and David L. Hall (New York, Ballantine, 2003). Chinese language translation as *Dao Buyuan Ren*.

Roger T. Ames (1947-) has retranslated many Chinese philosophical classics, hoping to disabuse Westerners of their misunderstandings in Chinese philosophy. Western researchers of Chinese philosophers, represented by those mentioned above, investigate Chinese philosophy with great profundity, and help Westerners to realize why Chinese philosophy should be properly recognized as "philosophy."

Whether Chinese or Western in descent, one must comprehend the *dao* of Chinese philosophers as experiential knowledge in order to understand truly the "Chinese philosophical sensibility."

Only by understanding this sensibility can one realize the essence of Chinese philosophy, and open up to the fascinating picture of Chinese philosophy as "philosophy." We must continue to promote the sustainment of "Chinese philosophical sensibility" through future generations in the context of Chinese-Western philosophical dialogue.

Appendix I:
Table of Key Philosophical Terms

Pinyin	Chinese	English
bore	般若	prajñ [Wisdom of the Buddha]
cheng	诚	creativity/sincerity
chengyi	诚意	concretizing one's mind
chenwei	谶纬	prophecy and apocrypha
dao	道	Dao, Tao, proper way, way-making
dazhuan	大传	*Great Appendix/Commentaries of Zhouyi*
de	德	excellence/virtue
duhua	独化	lone-transforming, transforms in solitude
fa	法	legal regulation, law, dharma, Dharma
fajie	法界	dharma realms
fuxing	复性	recovering nature
gewu	格物	investigation of things
guanxiang jici	观象系辞	observing image and attaching words
guayu	寡欲	diminishing one's desire
haoran zhiqi	浩然之气	great morale
huayan wujin yuanqi	华严无尽缘起	unending dependent co-arising of the Hua-yan school
ji	几	symptom of the intentional propensity
jian'ai	兼爱	universal love
jiayou	假有	revisionary beings
jieshen	戒慎	being concerned and anxious
junzi	君子	exemplary person
keji	克己	conquering oneself
keji fuli	克己复礼	disciplining the self and observing ritual propriety

kong	空	emptiness/sunyata
ming	命	destiny
ming	名	naming
neisheng waiwang	内 礻馔_	inner sage-outer king
nian	念	idea/intention/intentionality
qi	气	qi/psycho-material force
qiangao	谴告	heavenly condemnation
qingtan	清谈	pure or fine conversations
ren	仁	humanity, humane
shangtong	尚同	agreeing with a superior
shangxian		promoting the able
shen du	慎独	being alert of one's loneliness
shengrenzhidao	卜酥之道	the dao of sages
shi	势	propensity for power, powerful propensity, strategic propensity
shu	术	ruling strategy, statecraft
siduan	四端	the four moral sprouts/beginnings
siwen	斯文	this culture of ours
taiji	太极	Great Ultimate
taixu	太虚	Great Emptiness
tian	天	tian/heavens
tiandi zhixing	天地之性	pure good nature of heaven and earth
tianli	天理	heavenly patterns
tianming	天命	mandate of heavens
tianren ganying	天人感应	resonance between tian and human beings
tianzhi	天志	will of heavens
ti-yong	体用	body-function
wu	无	non-being, nothingness

wudai	无待	no reliance
wuming	无名	nameless
wuming	无明	darkness of ignorance (Avidya)
wunian	无念	non-intentionality
wuxing	五行	wuxing/five processes
xiao	孝	filial piety/family reverence/filial
xin	心	mind-heart, heart-mind, mind/heart
xing	性	xing/human nature/natural tendencies
xingkong	性空	being emptiness in nature
xingming zhixue	性命之学	learning about nature and destiny
xinshu	心术	mechanism of heart-mind
xu yi jing yin	虚一静因	unfilled, focused, pacified and temporized
xuanhe	玄合	mystically harmonious
xuanming zhijing	玄冥之境	dark remote setting
yi	意	intention/intentionality
yi	义	appropriate/appropriateness
yigen	意根	root of intentionality
yinian sanqian	一念三千	one intention contains three thousand suchnesses/worlds
yiwuguanwu	以物观物	vie w things from things themselves
yuanqi	缘起	dependent co-arising of different conditions
zhi liangzhi	致良知	extending one's continuous-experiencing
zhonghe	中和	focused and harmonious
ziran	自然	spontaneously so
zuowang	坐忘	quiet sitting and forgetting/forgetting oneself in quiet sitting

Appendix II:
Timeline of Chinese and Western Philosophies

Circa 11th century BC - King Wen of Zhou rearranged the Pre-Heavens Eight Trigrams of Fu Xi to be the Post-Heavens Eight Trigrams, and set the foundation for the philosophical spirit of Zhouyi, which is to "clarify human affairs by understanding the *dao* of *tian*."

Circa 600-500 BC - Laozi (Lao Dan) was active in this era. He wrote the *Daodejing*, which became the first classic of Daoism. Pythagoras of Samos (c. 580-c. 500 BC), the Greek philosopher and founder of the religious movement, lived around the same period.

Circa 551 BC - Confucius (Kong Qiu), the founder of Confucianism was born. His disciples collected and edited his thoughts and deeds into the *Analects*. The Greek philosopher Heraclitus (c. 540-c. 475 BC) was born and lived in Ephesus. He was active around 500 BC.

Circa 500 BC - Master Sun (Sun Wu) was active in this era. He was a great general and wrote *The Art of War*. Leucippus or Leukippos (first half of 5th century BC) was the first Greek to develop the theory of atomism.

Circa 475 BC - Mozi (Mo Di), the founder of Moism was born. Moism was as popular as Confucianism in Pre-Qin Era. His thought and activities can be found in the book Mozi. Socrates (c. 469-399 BC), a classical Greek philosopher was active around the same time.

Circa 372 BC - Mencius (Meng Ke) was born. He and his disciples wrote the book *Mencius*, and he was regarded as the "Second Confucius." Aristotle (384-322 BC) was a Greek philosopher, a student of Plato and teacher of Alexander the Great. By 335 BC he had returned to Athens, establishing his own school there known as the Lyceum.

Circa 369 BC - Zhuangzi (Zhuang Zhou) was born. He wrote the book Zhuangzi, which was the second foundational text of the Daoist philosophical and religious tradition. Its Inner Chapters is considered to contain his major thought. Pyrrho (c. 365-c. 275 BC), a Greek philosopher of classical antiquity, is credited as being the first Skeptic philosopher, and the inspiration for the school known as Pyrrhonism founded by Aenesidemus in the 1st century BC.

313 BC - Xunzi (Xun Kuang) was born. He wrote the book Xunzi and was regarded as another important Confucian philosopher. Zeno of Citium (c. 336-c. 264 BC), Greek philosopher, founder of Stoicism was active in an earlier time.

233 BC - Han Fei was jailed through a political intrigue and forced to commit suicide by taking poison in prison. The work bearing his name is a great synthesizer of legalism based on former legalists' thoughts on the powerful propensity, legal regulation and art of rulership.

134 BC - During the reign of Emperor Wu of the Han Dynasty, Dong Zhongshu persuaded him of the theory of resonance between *tian* and human beings. Hence, his *Three Recommendations on Heaven and Human Beings* (*tianren sance*) were accepted and transformed into state policy. This made Confucianism the dominant study and wiped out the other hundred schools. The Roman philosopher, statesman Marcus Tullius Cicero (106-43 BC) was active in a later time.

67 AD - Chinese Buddhist sutras first appeared around this year during the reign of Emperor Ming of Han Dynasty. Lucius Annaeus Seneca (c. 4 BC-65 AD), Roman Stoic

philosopher, statesman, dramatist, was active in this time.

79 AD - Emperor Zhang of the Han Dynasty summoned many Confucian scholars to meet in the Baihu Temple of Luoyang City. The *Memorandum of the Baihu Conference* (*Baihutongyi*) collected by Ban Gu inherited Dong Zhongshu's theory of the communication between *tian* and human beings. Its thoughts about "Three Ethical Guidelines (*san'gang*)" and "Six Ethical Principles (*liuji*)" had a far-reaching impact on traditional Chinese society.

249 - Wang Bi (226-249) died young in this year. He brought forth the metaphysical view that nothingness (*wu*) is the basis for beings (*you*) in his commentaries on the *Daodejing* and the *Book of Changes* (*Zhouyi*). Plotinus (c. 204-270) was a major philosopher of the ancient world who is widely considered to be the founder of Neoplatonism.

401 - Kumrajva arrived in Chang'an. He led his disciples to translate many Buddhist sutras. Since then the Chinese Buddhist interpretations of *sunyata* (emptiness) came closer to its original meaning. Among his disciples, Seng Zhao (384-414) was praised by him as the "greatest master of interpreting *sunyata*," and was regarded as the founder of the Chinese Buddhist philosophical system. Saint Augustine of Hippo (354-430), bishop and Doctor of the Church, is best known for his *Confessions* (401), his autobiographical account of his conversion.

629 - Xuan-zang left Chang'an to learn Indian Buddhism first hand. He brought back many Buddhist texts when he returned to China in 645. He devoted some twenty years to their translation, and became the founder of the Consciousness-only school of Chinese Buddhism.

638 - Hui-neng, the founder of Chinese Chan Buddhism and the sixth patriarch, was born. He was illiterate, but his

Platform Sutra of the Sixth Patriarch (*Tanjing*) was the only sutra (classic/*jing*) among Chinese Buddhist classics authored by Chinese monks.

772- Li Ao was born. As a student of Han Yu, Li Ao created a theory of recovering nature, which is the origin of several directions in Song-Ming epistemology.

1107 - Cheng Yi died. Before his death, Cheng was prosecuted and his school was labeled as a conspirator party. The Cheng Brothers were the founders of the School of Li of Song-Ming Neo-Confucianism. Cheng Yi's *Commentary on the Zhouyi* was very important in the theoretical School of Zhouyi. Anselm of Canterbury (c. 1033-1109) was an Italian, a Benedictine monk, a philosopher, and a prelate of the church who held the office of Archbishop of Canterbury from 1093 to 1109. Known as the founder of scholasticism, he is famous in the West as the originator of the ontological argument for the existence of God.

1175 - In the historical "E'hu Conference" in Jiangxi Province, Zhu Xi and Lu Jiuyuan debated over many important topics of Neo-Confucian philosophy.

1508 - Wang Yangming arrived at a remote area called Longchang in Guizhou province. During this low point in his life, he kept studying the *Book of Changes*, learning the wisdom of life from it. One night, he suddenly realized the *dao* of the sages and astonished his followers. This experience was regarded as "Sudden Enlightenment at Longchang." Martin Luther (1483-1546), a Christian theologian and Augustinian monk, initiated the Protestant Reformation.

1652 - Wang Fuzhi lived in seclusion and wrote his commentaries on *Zhouyi*, *Daodejing*, and other major philosophical classics. Before the introduction of Western philosophy, his philosophical system represented the highest achievement of traditional Chinese philosophy. Gottfried Wilhelm Leibniz (1646-1716) was a German philosopher, polymath and mathematician. He invented infinitesimal calculus independently of Newton, and he also invented the binary system. In philosophy, he was, along with René Descartes and Baruch Spinoza, one of the three greatest seventeenth-century rationalists and anticipated modern logic and analysis.

1919 - Hu Shi published his *An Outline of Chinese Philosophy*, of which he only finished the first half. This was the first history of Chinese philosophy with historical materials complied and interpreted according to the methodology of Western philosophy. British thinker Bertrand Russell (1872-1970) visited China in 1920.

1931 and 1934 - Fung Yu-lan completed *A History of Chinese Philosophy*, establishing a comprehensive system of Chinese philosophy.

1932 - Xiong Shili published *A New Treatise on the Consciousness-Only School*, which was considered to be a masterpiece in modern Chinese philosophy. German philosopher Martin Heidegger's *Being and Time* was published in 1927. It is his most important work and has profoundly influenced twentieth-century philosophy.

1957 - Tang Yongtong published his major works on the philosophy of Wei-Jin Dynasty. In 1954, French philosopher Michel Foucault served France as a cultural delegate to the University of Uppsala in Sweden.

1990 - After ten years of revision, Fung Yu-lan completed his 7-volume *New Version of the History of Chinese Philosophy*. The French philosopher Jacques Derrida (1930-2004) had a strong influence on Chinese academia. He visited China in 2001.

Appendix III:
Chronological Table of the Chinese Dynasties

The Paleolithic Period	c.1,700,000–10,000 years ago
The Neolithic Period	c. 10,000–4,000 years ago
Xia Dynasty	2070–1600 BC
Shang Dynasty	1600–1046 BC
Western Zhou Dynasty	1046–771 BC
Spring and Autumn Period	770–476 BC
Warring States Period	475–221 BC
Qin Dynasty	221–206 BC
Western Han Dynasty	206 BC–AD 25
Eastern Han Dynasty	25–220
Three Kingdoms	220–280
Western Jin Dynasty	265–317
Eastern Jin Dynasty	317–420
Northern and Southern Dynasties	420–589
Sui Dynasty	581–618
Tang Dynasty	618–907
Five Dynasties	907–960
Northern Song Dynasty	960–1127
Southern Song Dynasty	1127–1276
Yuan Dynasty	1276–1368
Ming Dynasty	1368–1644
Qing Dynasty	1644–1911
Republic of China	1912–1949
People's Republic of China	Founded in 1949